Elizabethan Hero

To order additional copies, please contact us.
BookSurge, LLC
www.booksurge.com
1-866-308-6235
orders@booksurge.com

Elizabethan Hero

The Life Of Sir Martin Frobisher

With best wishes

K. Frobisher

K A Frobisher

2005

Elizabethan Hero

CONTENTS

ACKOWLEDGEMENTS

It gives me great pleasure to acknowledge and to thank those that have supported and assisted me while researching and writing this book. I am especially thankful to my wife Eileen for her patience, help and encouragement and to my late father, George Frobisher, whose research has been invaluable. Also my thanks go to Hazel my daughter for her help with typing and my son Paul for his drawings. I am extremely grateful to Michael Barry who has written the forward and who has overseen and proofed my manuscript as well as being a kindly overseer and critic. Sheila Ambrose has painstakingly produced maps and drawings. I also thank the authorities at St Giles' Church, Cripplegate, London, All Saints Parish Church, Normanton, St Andrews Church, Plymouth, the Plymouth Reference Library and Plymouth Dome, the Public Records Office, Bristol, Natural Space Service & Heritage, Crozon, France and The National Trust.

The following have given permission for images to be used in the book and some are further mentioned in the caption accompanying the relevant illustration.

Bernard Finegan Gribble, *"Knighting the Captains on Board the Ark Royal"* 1936. Front cover detail and the whole painting by courtesy of The National Trust, Buckland Abbey and Sotheby's of London. Copyright Sotheby's of London

Cornelius Ketel, *"Portrait of Sir Martin Frobisher"*, 1577,

This book is dedicated to the memory of the author's father George Frobisher (1911—1997) without whose research and inspiration it would never have been written.

"Oh Frubysher Thy brute and name shall be enrolled in bookes,
That whosover after come and on thy labore lookes,
Shall muse and marvelle at thine actes, and the greatnesse of thy minde.
I say noe more lest some affirme, I fanne thy face with winde."

From "A welcome home to Mr Martin Frobysher" by Thomas Churchyard 1578

FOREWORD

This new and well-illustrated account of the life and achievements of the great Elizabethan adventurer, Sir Martin Frobisher, is to be warmly welcomed. It will be of particular interest to readers that the author of the present volume is a collateral descendant of Sir Martin Frobisher. The exploits of his contemporary, Sir Francis Drake, are well known. However, those of other seamen of his day have perhaps been less widely noticed.

This book will be especially welcome since we have recently celebrated other great English naval and military achievements including the victorious end of World War II and the 200th anniversary of Nelson's victory at Trafalgar.

The author gives a detailed account of the defeat of the Spanish Armada in 1588, placing special emphasis on the important and outstanding contribution of Sir Martin. Other lesser but significant naval activities continued for some time after that and ultimately, as the result of a small wound received in battle, he gave his life in the service of his country.

Importantly, the author gives the reader valuable coverage of a side of Frobisher's life which is less commonly remembered. He was one of those great English explorers who pushed out the boundaries of the then known world. In this case it was by his three epic voyages of discovery in which he sought what has come to be known as *The Northwest Passage*—a route around the north of Canada into the Pacific Ocean. Remarkably, these three exploratory journeys appear in many ways to have been better organised and to some degree more successful than nineteenth century attempts in the same region. The Northwest Passage, our author tells us, was Frobisher's "chief passion". The risks involved at that time in such a voyage into a very hostile environment and the courage and determination which Frobisher and his crews displayed can only fill us with admiration today.

Frobisher was clearly a man with great gifts of leadership and a sense of the value and importance of team work and the welfare of his men. This led him to go to great lengths and to take serious personal risks to seek out men who had been separated from their companions by storms and other dangers. He demanded high standards from his men and demonstrated a very practical ability in setting before them the moral standards of the Christian faith, which he expected to be followed during his voyages. Sir Martin Frobisher's efforts both as an explorer and in his naval service brought him warm personal commendation from Queen Elizabeth herself. He is an Englishman who deserves much wider recognition and it is therefore with a sense of great satisfaction that I commend this new biography to the reader.

Michael V Barry (October 2005)
Sometime Senior Lecturer in English,
The Queen's University of Belfast.

INTRODUCTION

In writing this biography of Sir Martin Frobisher I have fulfilled a long-standing ambition. As a young boy I attended Kirkham Grammar School in Lancashire where I learnt about the Elizabethan Age in history lessons. I remember being stirred and intrigued by the stories of Elizabeth's "seadogs" and especially about the one bearing my own surname and his involvement in the epic battle against the Spanish Armada. Was I descended from him? My father George Frobisher shared the same inquisitiveness in his youth and, when he semi-retired in 1972 he began a long and painstaking research project into his family tree. He produced a magnificent piece of work and traced the family back to 1255AD, to John Frobysler of Chirk in North Wales. He established that no one could be directly descended from Sir Martin as he had no sons but he, and therefore I am collateral descendant of his brother Davey. My father died in 1997 and left me his research papers, requesting that I continue where he had left off. He gave instructions that his finished work was to be placed on permanent loan in the reference library of Huddersfield University. He was very keen that future researchers into the Frobisher family or other interested parties should benefit by having access to it.

In setting out to write this biography, I have been very conscious of my own limitations as an author and I merely ask the reader to bear with me and with any errors or omissions that I may have made. I have not sought to describe in detail the social, economic or political trends of Elizabethan times except when they help us to understand the life and exploits of Sir Martin. Neither have I tried to do justice to other great seamen of those times. Others have achieved that for most of them. The focus of this biography is Sir Martin. I hope I have not been too biased, but I believe that he has often been overlooked and his contributions downplayed. Those traits in his character that were strong, bold and aggressive and sometimes considered coarse have often been exaggerated to the detriment of other traits that enabled him to be an outstanding leader amongst men. It was only because he possessed such powerful personal qualities that he was able to achieve all that he did to further the reputation and influence of England. There is no doubt that history shows conclusively that it was men like Sir Martin Frobisher, with all their faults and failings, who displayed amazing acts of heroism during Elizabeth's reign and who laid the foundations of England as we know it today. His fame as an explorer and navigator, his courage and skill as a seaman and admiral have given him a distinguished position in English maritime history. He was indeed an Elizabethan hero, as his story will show.

Portrait of Sir Martin Frobisher by Cornelius Ketel 1577

CHAPTER I

ROOTS AND CHILDHOOD

The Frobishers, according to the Harleian Manuscripts, are descended from John Frobysler of Flintshire in North Wales. He was of Scottish extraction and could possibly have come from the Forbes clan which was sometimes known as "Forbois". It is quite likely that the clan's name is derived from the old gaelic word "Forba" meaning field or district and the Pictish word "ais" which means place. This could be the derivation of the surname Frobysler. Another theory is that the surname could be derived from the French word "fourbisseur" meaning sword cutler. Others have suggested that it derives from "furbisher", a polisher of armour and chain-mail. The definitive meaning will probably remain a mystery, as it is difficult to be absolutely certain because of the passage of time. It is also interesting to note that there have been many different spellings of the surname through the years, probably because it was written phonetically in a time when literacy was quite rare and spellings were still unstable. The surname has many variants e.g. Frobysler, Frobyser, Frobysher, Ffrubisher, Frobishaw, Forbisher, etc.

John Frobysler was born about 1255 AD. and went to England to serve in King Edward I army in his wars against the Welsh at the turn of the 13th Century. For his services he was granted lands in or near to Chirk in North Wales. The castle at Chirk is still in excellent condition and stands as an impressive reminder of the conflicts of that era.

Chirk Castle, North Wales.

Ruins of Central Courtyard, Holt Castle, North Wales.

It was John's great great grandson John, born about 1370, who was first to settle in Yorkshire. He married Cecilye, daughter of John Andrew of Holt Castle, which is situated in an idyllic spot by the River Dee just a few miles north of Chirk. He and his wife moved from Chirk to the Pontefract area of Yorkshire. This was probably because of the fact that many Yorkshire men had gone to serve in King Edward's army. Among them was Henry de Laci, the Earl of Lincoln, and baron of Pontefract in Yorkshire. He was one of Edward's chief commanders and it was on his estates around Pontefract that John Frobyser settled. His grandson John Frobysher, born about 1440, married Joan, daughter of Sir William Scargill who according to the Correspondence of Sylvanus Urban was the "Seneschal" (steward) of Pontefract Castle and head of one of the most famous knightly houses of Yorkshire. So it was that by the 16th Century the family were classed as Gentlemen and occupied an important position in the County. Martin Frobisher, the great grandson of John was born in 1535 at Altofts near Normanton in Yorkshire. His father was Barnard Frobysher and his mother was Margaret the daughter of Sir John York of Gowthwaite.

Martin's family tree is as follows:

John Frobysler (c.1255) of Flint of Chirke and Scotland

John Frobyser (c.1280) of Chirke m Jane Deghan of Wripham

John Frobyser (c.1310) of Chirke m Elizabeth dau. of Thomas Bulkeley of Beaumaris

Thurstan Frobyser (c.1340) of Chirke m Grace dau. of John Hyde of Hyde, Cheshire

John Frobyser (c.1370) of Chirke & Altofts m Cecilye dau. of John Andrew, Holt Castle

Thurstan Frobyser (c.1400) of Chirke & Altofts m Jane dau. of John Pierce

John Frobysher (c 1440) of Altofts m Joan dau. of Sir William Scargill

John Frobysher (Buried 1544) of Altofts m Katherine
dau. of Robert Drax
Barnard Frobysher (buried 1542) m Margaret dau. of
Sir John Yorke
Martin Frobisher (1535) m Isabel Riggatt of Snaith
(1559 died 1588)
m Dame Dorothy Wentworth dau. of Lord Wentworth 1591

Martin's father Barnard was a gentleman of some stature.
He was churchwarden of Normanton Parish Church in 1537
and Bailiff at Hetton and Batley. The family held their own coat
of arms which was granted to Francis of Doncaster in 1550 and
was also used by Sir Martin. It is described as "ermine on a fess,
engrailed between three griffins' heads erased sable, a greyhound
courant, argent, collared gules".

Unfortunately Barnard and Margaret both died when quite
young: Barnard in 1542 and Margaret in 1549. Martin therefore
was orphaned at 14 years of age and as there were no schools in
the area (probably because of the dissolution of the monasteries)
Martin was sent to London to be cared for by his uncle, Sir John
York. According to the merchant Michael Lok, Sir John noticed
that the youth was "of great spirit and bould courage and natu-
rall hardness of body"[1] (see endnotes) and so the young, strong
and adventurous Martin was sent to sea.

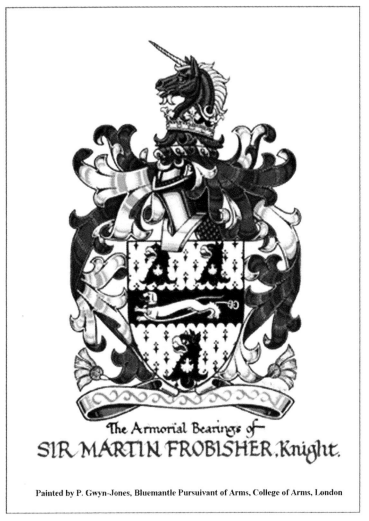

The Armorial Bearings of
SIR MARTIN FROBISHER, Knight.

Painted by P. Gwyn-Jones, Bluemantle Pursuivant of Arms, College of Arms, London

Sir Martin Frobisher's Coat of Arms.

CHAPTER 2

MARTIN'S EARLY VOYAGES

Sir John York, as Master of the Queen's Mint, was involved in most of the trading ventures of that time, especially those sailing to the west coast of Africa. It was not surprising therefore that Martin's first voyage was on board one of the ships of the Wyndham expedition, which went to trade with Guinea in West Africa in 1553. A Portuguese man, Anthonie Pinteado, was captain of one of the ships. He was chosen because he was already well acquainted with the seas of that region but despite this, and early in the voyage, Captain Wyndham unilaterally took over the command of the expedition and demoted Pinteado. Not content with the gold already received from trade in Guinea, he decided to sail further down the coast for a load of peppers. Pinteado was ordered to take his ship up a river and 80 tons of peppers were loaded in 60 days. Meanwhile the other ships remained at anchor at the river's mouth. Here, because of the oppressive heat and tropical diseases, the men on board the ships began to die at the alarming rate of 4 or 5 per day. Wyndham also died. Pinteado, oblivious of this further delayed his return from upstream because of the abundant supply of peppers he was loading. When he did return, the crews were so angry with him because his prolonged delay had caused so much suffering and death, that they forcefully restrained him and put him in the boys' quarters as a punishment. He died of fever six days after their departure from that terrible place. 140 men set out on the voyage. Only about 40 were fortunate enough to return to Plymouth, and among them was Martin Frobisher. It must have been quite a voyage for a young boy.

The gold and pepper made that first voyage extremely profitable and Sir George Barne, Sir John York, Thomas Lok, Anthony Hickman and Edward Castelin planned another voyage the following year. John Lok, brother of Thomas, was captain and the young Martin went along too. When they arrived at Guinea, Martin went ashore as a pledge for trade. Unfortunately he was taken captive and imprisoned. Later he wrote a declaration to the Privy Council explaining how he was held in the Castle of Myne for nine months. It appears that a local chief detained Martin after the English ships had to leave suddenly because a Portuguese brig arrived and opened fire on them. Martin had to be left behind and was handed over to the Portuguese. His nine month's captivity was not too onerous and he was probably freed as a result of negotiations (and no doubt at his uncle's expense) which later took place between the Portuguese and English.

In 1559 Martin went on a voyage to the Barbary Coast off North West Africa and was also involved in a venture to capture the Portuguese Castle of Mina in Guinea. This was disguised as a trading enterprise but the pirate Strangeways and his companions, including Martin, were arrested and tried. From 1563 to 1573 he was closely associated with the two Hawkins, Killigrew, Erizye, Lane, Morgan, Chichester and Vaughan; and in such company there can be little doubt as to his occupation. He was busy capturing ships and their cargoes that belonged, or were supposed to belong, to Catholics. By 1564 the name and reputation of Martin Frobisher as a privateer or pirate was as well known to Philip of Spain and as equally hated as that of John Hawkins.

At this time Elizabeth was at war with the Catholic party in France and English privateers were licensed to go against their ships. John Appleyard of Yorkshire fitted out 3 vessels for this purpose, the *John Appleyard*, the *Anne Appleyard* and the *Elizabeth Appleyard*. Martin was captain of the *Anne*, his brother John Frobisher was captain and half owner of the *John*, and the Cornish rover Peter Killigrew was captain of the *Elizabeth*. They put to sea and returned to Plymouth with five French ships as prizes. They were arrested but rode to London and, with the aid of Davey (David) Frobisher, they were released. In 1565 Martin was cruising in the *Mary Flower* and captured the *Flying Spirit*, a Spanish ship laden with a rich cargo of cochineal. He also captured a Flemish ship called the *White Unicorn*. It is obvious that he was not always particular about the nationality of the ships he captured. He was again arrested for piracy in 1565 but was released from prison in 1566, on condition that he did not go to sea without a proper licence. He therefore took on a legitimate localised role and became captain of the *Mary Flower*, a ship that had been fitted out for carrying coal. She was loaded in Newcastle and various ports in Yorkshire and the coal was then shipped to other parts of the country.

Martin eventually secured a licence from Cardinal Chastillon, which commissioned him to capture French ships belonging to the Catholic enemies of the Prince of Conde. In 1568, along with others, he brought captured ships back to Aldeburgh in Suffolk. In 1569 he was off Rye, on the South East Coast of England, commanding two "tall and well armed ships". He probably still held the licence from Cardinal Chastillon and had also been commissioned by the Prince of Orange to capture Spanish ships. The merchants of Rye were alarmed because they thought their ships, which carried goods for French Protestants, might fall prey to Martin Frobisher's ships and so they wrote to the Privy Council seeking protection. The Cinque Ports had a commission from the Queen to fit out ships specifically prepared for their protection from pirates but the Rye men told the Council that "no six ships were fit to cope with Frobisher". Martin was gaining quite a reputation for his privateering expertise. Later in 1569 he chased and captured a French ship, the *Marie*, with a cargo of wines. He was sued by the owners and then arrested at Aldeburgh in Suffolk while in possession of yet another prize, the *Madeleine*. The court decided that the ship and its cargo were to be restored to their owner and Martin was imprisoned, under sentence to pay £900. A Mr Bowes, who had helped him previously, paid his fine, claimed Martin's ship and then sold it to Lady Elizabeth Clinton, the wife of the Lord High Admiral.

There was a lot of politicking during those times because of the fractious relations between states in Europe and the next we hear of Martin he is in the Queen's service capturing foreign vessels, especially those from France and Portugal. It was perceived that Elizabeth's realm was threatened by the opposition to her reign in Ireland and the possibility of an enemy using Ireland as a base from which to attack the mainland of England. In 1571, Edward Horsey wrote to Lord Burghley informing him that a ship was being fitted out for Martin Frobisher at Portsmouth. It was to be used as a supply ship in Elizabeth's plans to extinguish the threat to her from Ireland. The ship was probably the *Carrick Lane*. For the next few years Martin was engaged in this enterprise, while at the same time he used any opportunity which presented itself to capture foreign vessels and their cargoes. In November 1573 he seized the *Clock* and brought her back to port as a prize and was subsequently summoned to appear before the Council to account for his piratical actions. This is the last known record of his activities as a privateer, pirate or sea rover and it is difficult to know whether his actions had always been legal or not. He was arrested three or four times on the charge of piracy but he never seems to have been convicted of an offence. Soon after his acquittal he was nearly always given a further commission, either from a foreign prince or from the Queen. Several of the ships which he brought home as prizes were soon returned to their owners and it seems that Elizabeth or her Council did not look upon his activities with disfavour.

In 1572 and 1573 Martin was involved in some of the political intrigues of the time. He went along with Gerald Fitzgerald, the Earl of Desmond, in his attempt to escape back to Ireland. The Earl was an Irish patriot on bail, on suspicion of treason. The attempt was betrayed, whether by Martin or others we cannot be sure. The second episode was when Stukeley, (the cousin of Sir John Hawkins), "a bold freebooter, ready to undertake any service which would yield him ample reward"[2], entered the service of the King of Spain and was trying to raise an army to invade Ireland. In England, there were those who were seeking support from the Catholics and others who were discontented with Elizabeth. Martin's wife helped to thwart this plot. The affair is sometimes referred to as the occasion when Martin duped King Philip of Spain. The evidence is rather against this, although Sir John Hawkins, Martin's comrade, was well known for this sort of thing and it could be that he was the one responsible.

CHAPTER 3

THE FIRST ARCTIC VOYAGE—1576

The sixteenth century was a time of European worldwide exploration. Explorers had gone South, East and West but very little was known of the Northern Seas, especially to the Northwest. Interest in exploring this region had developed over the years. Henry the seventh had sponsored an expedition to the northern seas in 1496 and John Cabot had sailed from Bristol with a crew of eighteen men in the *Matthew*. They reached the coast of North America, probably Newfoundland or Nova Scotia, thought it was Asia and took formal possession of it for England. Other expeditions followed from Bristol and hopes were high of finding a sea route around the North of the Americas to Cathay (China) and the East. Henry the Eighth became interested in what had become known as "The Northwest Passage" and in May 1527 he sent the *Samson* and *Mary of Gilford* in search of it. They left Plymouth and sailed north and west into the Arctic waters but there the *Samson* foundered and, afraid of the terrible weather conditions and the pack ice, the expedition returned home.

Martin's interest in the Northwest Passage became his chief passion. George Best confirms this when he wrote, "Long time he (Martin) conferred with his private friendes of these secretes, and made also manye offers for performing of the same in effect with sundry merchants of our countrey, above fifteen yeares before he attempted the same".[3] So Martin, from when he was aged about twenty, had been trying to find the means to go on a voyage to the Arctic in search of the Northwest Passage. He began conversations with a merchant called Michael Lok, in which he mooted the idea and it was Lok who became the prime mover of the enterprise. Before anything else could be done they had to get a licence which authorised them to embark on such a voyage. At that time it was the Muscovy Company that had the sole rights to explore the Northern Seas but they had confined their sphere of activity to the Northeast and were trading with Russia. They had not thus far ventured to the Northwest into the Arctic region. Eventually they were persuaded to grant a licence.

A typical 16th Century merchant's house, Plymouth.

A model of a merchant planning a voyage with a navigator in the 16th Century.

The next step was to raise funds. Not many investors were willing to put money into such an uncertain venture and only £875 was raised. Lok by now was so committed to the project that he decided to underwrite all other expenses. A new ship called the *Gabriel* was built and another called the *Michael* bought. They weighed about 20 tons and 25 tons respectively and a small 7 to 10 ton pinnace was also built for the voyage. A pinnace was a small boat with oars and sails that acted as a tender for larger vessels. They were used to ferry people between ships and from the larger ships to the land when the sea was too shallow or too dangerous for them to approach. They were also used to tow the larger sailing ships when there was little or no wind or when leaving a harbour.

A replica of the *Golden Hind* in Brixham Harbour, Devon. Typical of a 16th Century ship.

Having made all preparations, the fleet was ready to sail on 7th June 1576. They sailed from Radcliffe on the Thames with Martin as admiral and pilot, Christopher Hall as captain of the *Gabriel* and Griffyn Owen as captain of the *Michael.* The total crew numbered 35. As they sailed along the Thames they passed Greenwich and the Queen and her court waved them farewell and the ships responded by firing their guns in salute. After leaving the Thames estuary they sailed north, calling at the Shetlands to repair a leak in the *Michael.* They then set course for the Northwest and sailed into the jaws of a very severe storm, a harbinger of things to come. The pinnace was totally overcome by the raging sea and foundered with the loss of four men. After a fruitless search to find and rescue them the ships sailed on. As they approached Greenland they became separated. The crew of the *Michael*, so they said afterwards, tried to find the *Gabriel* for 4 days but were unsuccessful, so Captain Owen turned for home, fearful of the ice and the appalling weather. They arrived back at London on 1st September 1576 and reported that the *Gabriel* was lost with all hands.

The Gabriel was not lost and Martin had bravely sailed on with his remaining 18 men. After 3 days they sighted the coast of Greenland but couldn't find a landing place. This was because of pack ice and the huge icebergs that were being driven by the wind and currents along the coastline. They sailed on and soon found themselves enveloped in a dense fog. They successfully came through it and rejoiced at seeing the coastline again because it enabled them take their bearings and have a sense of direction. Their relief was short lived for almost immediately a violent storm arose and the *Gabriel* was tossed about with such force that she was like a cork in the raging ocean. At one stage she listed so badly that the mountainous waves began rushing in amidships and one huge wave caught the foresail and swept it over the ship's side. As the sail was dragged through the water alongside the ship it caused her to list so badly that she was in imminent danger of capsizing. The crew feared for their lives but Martin, with huge strength and agility, rescued the situation as he risked his life to release the foresail and to cut off the mizzenmast. One can only imagine what it must have been like to carry out this amazing feat while the wind was tearing at him and the ship was heaving and rolling on the angry ocean. The result was that the ship was partly righted but as she rolled from side to side the water that had entered her decks was emptied overboard sweeping away many valuable articles with it. Thus by an act of extreme bravery and at personal risk of losing his own life the ship and the crew were saved from going down into the icy waters.

Most men, after such harrowing experiences, would have set sail for home. Martin, not to be deflected from the purpose of the voyage, sailed on; he was absolutely determined to find the Northwest Passage, if it existed. On 28th July they sighted land and mistakenly thought it was the coast of Labrador but in fact it was the southern end of Baffin Island. It has to be remembered that in the 16th Century this part of the world was almost uncharted and they only had very vague maps and charts to help their navigation. As they passed into the straits they encountered huge icebergs which towered over them and which were being driven about by wind and currents. The men's courage and seamanship, negotiating such dangerous hazards in a small wooden sailing ship and in unknown territory without accurate charts to guide them is amazing.

They sailed on for 16 days until the seas were clear of ice and they were able to land on various islands. One they named "Hall's Island", after the captain. Here they were able to repair the leaks in the ship's hull, which had been caused by contact with the ice. On 11th August, as they sailed in the strait, they named it "Frobisher's Straits". They thought at the time that it was the passage that would lead them around the north of America. The straits around the south of America had been named after their discoverer Magellan, so they decided it was fitting that the straits around the north should also be named after their discoverer. They were convinced (quite wrongly of course) that the land to their left was America and the land to their right was Asia.

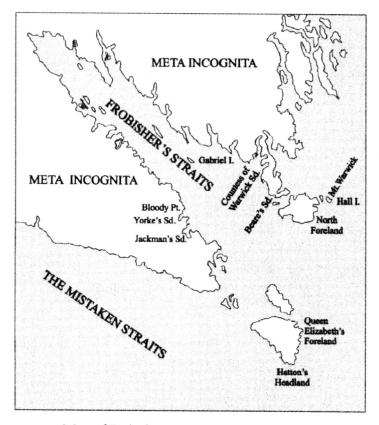

Map of Frobisher Straits Area, Baffin Island.

On 19th August Martin, with the captain and six or eight men, launched a small boat and landed on Burcher's Island. They climbed to a high vantagepoint from where they could view the whole area. Suddenly in the distance they saw seven small boats paddling towards them. After returning to their ship Martin sent some of his men ashore to befriend these strangers in their little boats. Eventually some of them were coaxed to come aboard and Martin and his men welcomed them with friendly gestures and gave them presents. One of the Eskimos (they are now correctly called Inuit) by his gestures seemed to be offering himself to act as a guide to lead them through the straits. They interpreted the sign language to mean that he would paddle his boat (kayak) ahead of them and that if they followed him they would be through the straits in two days. He was then sent ashore accompanied by five of Martin's men. Very concerned for their safety, Martin gave them very strict orders not to go out of sight of the ship. The five men set down their passenger near to where he had left his kayak, and then they rowed off and followed him until they all disappeared round a headland. The five men were never to be seen again.

An Inuit Male by John White.

Martin sailed slowly along the coastline searching for his lost men. He had the trumpet blown and the ship's guns fired, but it was all to no avail. He deliberately shot the ship's cannon over the tops of the Inuit houses so as not to harm the occupants, but just to warn them to return his five men. He searched diligently all the next day but there was still no sign of them. In despair, presuming that his men had been captured and imprisoned, he sailed on to search for other Inuit. His intention was to capture some of them and then to hold them as hostages so that they could be released in exchange for his men. After 3 days he had not found any and so he returned along the coast to where the Inuit houses were, only to find that the Inuit and their houses had all disappeared. If the 5 men were with them and were still alive they had been forcefully taken away. The five men were never seen again. Just why they disobeyed orders and went out of sight of the ship will never be known, but Martin never gave up hope of finding them.

Without the small pinnace it was usually far too dangerous for Martin to try to go ashore and so he hadn't collected any tokens of possession for Elizabeth and England. He was in something of a quandary. He needed tokens from these new lands to prove his discoveries. However as they sailed on some Inuit kayaks were spotted and they approached the *Gabriel*. Martin was still anxious to take some hostages to exchange for his missing men. As the Inuit came alongside Martin and his crew tried to grab some of them but they always managed to dodge their efforts and avoid capture. Then Martin found a shiny brass bell and offered it to one of them. The Inuit was sorely tempted and could not resist the urge to possess it and in his efforts to get the bell he came far too close to the *Gabriel's* side. In a flash Martin grabbed hold of the man's wrist with a steely grip and in one jerking movement of brute strength he yanked the man aboard while he was still sitting in his kayak. He had his hostage. Would the Inuit release his men in exchange for their friend? The Englishmen waited in hope but the wait proved fruitless. The Inuit didn't return and the hope of an exchange faded. Having only thirteen men left and with winter approaching, Martin reluctantly decided to set sail for home. He departed from Baffin Island on 26th August and arrived back in London on 9th October. One can imagine the joyful reunion with the *Michael's* crew who had given up all hope of ever seeing the *Gabriel* or her crew again. For Martin and his men there was nothing but great admiration for completing an amazing voyage of discovery and for "Bringing with them their strange man and his bote, which was of such wonder onto the whole city and to the rest of the realm that heard of yt as seemed never to have happened the like great matter to any man's knowledge". [4]

While the first voyage did not end in discovering or sailing through a Northwest Passage to the East, it had been encouraging and it was generally believed that Martin had found the Passage even if he had not gone through it. However there now followed a turn of events which would divert Martin from his longstanding goal. He passed on the things they had collected during the voyage including the tokens of possession. Amongst these was a piece of rock. The story is told that one of the sailors' wives threw a piece of this rock on the fire and when it was very hot she threw some vinegar on it. The result was that it glittered with golden specks. Were the golden specks real gold? It was taken to a London assayer for tests and he confirmed that it did indeed contain a high yield of gold.

A more probable account of what really happened is that Lok felt the rock to be very heavy for normal rock and so he had it assayed for precious metals. The Crown's assayers told him that it did not contain gold but Lok was obsessed and eventually an assayer named John Baptista Agnello convinced him that there was gold in the "ore". When asked how he had found gold when others had not, he replied "It is necessary to know how to flatter nature". Alarm bells should have been ringing but the allure of gold silenced them. Lok decided to apply to the Queen for a licence to send another expedition to bring back more of the rock, which for him had become "ore". A licence was granted and with the rumours of gold abroad it was not difficult to finance and prepare a second voyage. Martin must have believed what he was told concerning the gold in the "ore" and agreed to lead a second expedition.

CHAPTER 4

THE SECOND ARCTIC VOYAGE—1577

On 17th March 1577 the Cathay Company was formed, with the approval of the Crown. Lok, Martin Frobisher and all those involved in the first voyage were admitted to the Company. Lok was appointed as the Company's Governor and Martin was appointed as the High Admiral of all seas and waters, countries, lands and isles, as well as Cathay and all other countries and places that he might discover. Queen Elizabeth, not to miss out where gold was involved, backed the enterprise with £1000. She also loaned a 200 ton ship called the *Ayde*, which could carry many tons of "ore", to sail with the *Michael* and *Gabriel*. The ships were manned with 120 men; 90 sailors, gunners, carpenters etc. and 30 miners, refiners and merchants. Supplies to last 7 months were loaded on board. On their journey north they were to transport 6 criminals to Friesland where they were to befriend the inhabitants and report back on how they had fared among them.

Martin's orders were to proceed directly to Hall's Island to mine the "ore" and load it aboard the *Ayde*. While this was being done he was to take the smaller ships to search for his five lost men and also to make further discoveries to ascertain whether there was a passage to the Far East. He was to ensure however that he was back by the time the *Ayde* was loaded and ready for the return journey. The ships left Backwall, on the Thames, on 26th May 1577. They called at Harwich in Essex to put ashore surplus persons on board. The Queen had left letters aboard ship commanding that no more than 120 men were to be taken (Martin had 134 men on board and so 14 had to be put ashore). They sailed on and on 7th June spent a day at the Orkneys. After loading more provisions they sailed Northwest for 16 days, during which time they were out of sight of land. On 4th July they arrived at Friesland, ("Friesland" was mistaken for an island in the North Atlantic. In fact we now know it was the eastern coast of Greenland. The only map that Martin had was Zeno's sea card, which had many errors on it). They sailed along the coastline for 4 days encountering huge icebergs which, they noted, were formed from fresh water and had far more mass below the water than above it. Some of the icebergs were over half a mile in circumference. After safely passing through these ice-infested waters they set course for Frobisher's Straits. As soon as they arrived a great storm descended on them during which the *Michael* was badly damaged. Her steering was smashed and her topmasts broken off and blown overboard. The other ships became separated from each other. The captains and their crews had to fight desperately to keep their ships from being overwhelmed by the raging seas. When the storm had abated they were very fortunate to have survived and one by one they were all reunited. On 17th July they sighted land and were much relieved when it proved to be Hall's Island, their destination.

Martin took some men ashore in one of the pinnaces to look for "ore" and to test it. They found none. The records of Best and Settle (one of the merchants on board) testify that these venturers believed sincerely in their Christian faith and the providence of God. Best writes,

"…He (*Martin*) could not gette in all that Iland a peece fo bigge as a walnut, where the firfte was found, fo that it may feeme a great miracle of God, that being only one rich Ftone in all the Iland, the fame fhould be found by one of our Countreyman, whereby it Fhoulde appeare, God's diuine will and pleafure is, to haue oure common wealth encreafed with no leffe abundance of his hydden treafures and gold mynes, than any other nation, and would, that the fayth of his Gofpell and holy name fhould be publifhed and enlarged thoughe all thofe corners of the earth, amongeft, thofe Idolatrous Infidels".[5]

After a search on other islands they found the "ore" in abundance, which rather nullifies Best's comments.

On Friday 19th July Martin set off for the shore with some of his men but when approaching the shore he found he couldn't land anywhere because of the expanse of ice between them and the shore. He had to go as far as Hall's Island before he could find a suitable place and having gone ashore he and his men climbed a hill and erected a cairn. He had a trumpet sounded and then, as they all knelt around the cairn with the flag of St George flying, he prayed and named the place Mount Warwick. As they were returning to their boats they happened to look back and to their surprise they could see a number of Inuit on the top of Mount Warwick, which they had only just left. They were shouting and waving and jumping about and clearly wanted to talk. They retraced their steps and having reached the spot Martin sent two of his men to meet with two of theirs. They met them very cautiously and traded a few small items but there was insufficient trust between them to go any further than that. As Martin's men withdrew and were nearing their boats, the

Inuit followed them and became even more agitated, so Martin and the captain went to speak with them. If the opportunity presented itself Martin fully intended to capture two of them, so that he could take them back to the ship, where they would have been well treated. His plan was to give one of them some toys, trinkets and clothing so that he could take them back to his friends. Martin hoped that this would show the Inuit that he wanted to have a friendly relationship with them. The other one he intended to keep so that he could act as an interpreter for further conversations.

As Martin and the captain were bartering with the Inuit they suddenly pounced on two of them and tried to hold them. The Inuit escaped their grasp and ran away. They quickly recovered their bows and arrows and pursued the unarmed Martin and the captain, shooting arrows at them all the time. Unfortunately for Martin a well-aimed arrow implanted itself in one of his buttocks. The excruciating pain from the wound almost disabled him but he staggered along as best and as fast as he could. His pursuers were rapidly gaining on him and if it had not been for his men running pell-mell from the boats to rescue him he would certainly have met with a violent and untimely death. They gave chase to the perpetrators who had almost relieved them of their Admiral. In the scuffle that followed, a Cornishman called Nicholas Conger, an excellent runner and wrestler, caught an Inuit and wrestled him to the ground and "made his side ache for a month". [6] All the others escaped and ran away. Martin and his men returned to their boat with their captive, (there is no record of what they did about the arrow in Martin's buttock) and then set off to return to the fleet. Another violent storm suddenly arose and they had to seek shelter. They spent a wet, cold and very miserable night, having managed to land on another island. The same storm was buffeting the *Ayde* and the other ships to such an extent that it was not safe to remain static and so they had no alternative but to weigh anchor. All the time they were in the Sound they were in great peril from the icebergs, which were being blown hither and thither, often striking and scraping along the sides of the ships. Others missed by inches and the crews used all their ingenuity and all sorts of methods to push the icebergs away from the ship's hulls so that they could not damage them or even worse, pierce them. To add to their alarm a fire suddenly broke out on board the *Ayde* but mercifully it was soon spotted and extinguished by the crew. Very fortunately the captains spied a small patch of clear water in the distance where there was very little ice. To reach it however they had to tack 14 times in 32 hours, which was an amazing feat of endurance and seamanship. The dangers they faced at that time cannot be overstated. Floating icebergs, some huge and some small surrounded them and all were capable at any moment of holing any of the ships and sinking them.

On 21st July Martin returned to the ships and they all gave thanks to God for their deliverance from the perils they had just faced. After that experience Martin was not at all happy with the safety of that anchorage and so he gave orders to set sail for the southern coast of the straits. They came upon a bay, which was more sheltered and provided a safer harbour. Martin took a pinnace and landed on a small island close by. The cliffs and sands glistened as if the whole island were made of gold. The assayers tested the rocks but were disappointed when they found no evidence of precious metals in them. They recollected the proverb "All that glitters is not gold".

On 23rd July Martin and 70 men landed on the southern shore, presuming it to be the continent of America. They assembled at the blast of a trumpet and on their knees thanked God for his protecting hand and for granting them the honour of making such discoveries, which would greatly advantage their Queen and England. After marching around the area for about 5 miles they returned to the ships so that the mining of the "ore" could begin. They had found a rich deposit closeby and the miners got busy and had soon quarried 20 tons. Meanwhile the wind and tide were forcing large quantities of ice into the sound where they were anchored and the fleet was once again in great peril. Just in time to prevent the ships being crushed, a huge iceberg, carried along by the wind, beached itself on the shore and thus provided a very effective temporary shelter. Even then the danger was very real and they had to escape before disaster overtook them. There was no time to lose and consequently they had to leave the 20 tons of "ore" on the shore. They embarked and sailed away to another island where there was a much safer anchorage. While exploring this island they came across some scattered human bones and after examining them they came to the conclusion that whoever they belonged to, he or she must have been killed and eaten by the Inuit. Their captive contradicted this idea and told them by signs that wolves or some other creature would have killed him. They also found at the site articles that must have belonged to the deceased. There was a lot of fish, which had been hidden under some stones to protect it from scavengers, some sleds, bridles, fish skin kettles, bone knives and other items used by the Inuit. Their captive then put a quickly made bridle on to one of the dogs, attached the other end to one of the sleds, jumped on and demonstrated how it was used. This proved to the men that the Inuit used dog sleds just as English people back at home used horses and carriages.

On 29th July they anchored in Countess of Warwick Sound, which proved to be the most favourable harbour they had found so far. On an island close by they found large deposits of "ore" which, when washed, glistened with golden specks. Martin immediately set the miners to work. He joined them and showed that he was a strong workman as well as a good general. By this example he encouraged all the men, as well as the miners, to get busy with the heavy work involved. As the mining work proceeded others discovered a number of Inuit houses on the island and from their contents learned much about their occupants' way of life. Their houses, built under the ground so as to insulate them from the cold, were round and constructed with whalebones covered with sealskins. They were obviously a nomadic people and existed by hunting. It was from here that the captive Inuit made a signal to his friends, who were nearby, that he was being held because of the 5 men they had captured on the first voyage. He obviously knew what had happened to the men but didn't reveal it. He merely denied that they had been killed and eaten.

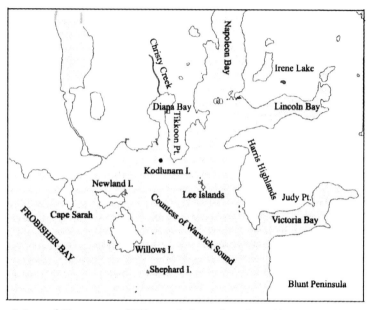

Map of Countess of Warwick Sound and Kodlunarn Island.

On 31ˢᵗ July the *Michael* and *Ayde* returned from the southern coast and anchored in Countess of Warwick Sound with the others. The day before, they had seen about 20 Inuit men in a large boat and had tried to make friendly contact with them but they paddled away at great speed and could not be caught. Captain Yorke of the *Michael* had seen some tents off Yorke Sound and went to investigate. He found, amongst other things, some canvas, a shirt, a girdle and 3 shoes of various sizes. He was convinced they belonged to the 5 missing men. Leaving a note for the captives in case they should ever return there and leaving some items as tokens of their friendly intent, he then set off to find the Inuit in case they still held the men. Having told the crew of the *Ayde* what they had discovered, the two crews joined forces. They set off in 2 pinnaces for the place where the tents had been seen. A number of men were landed some distance from the tents so that they could approach from behind and prevent any escape inland. When the main party arrived at the place where the tents had been seen the night before, they found that the tents had gone. The other party, while marching over the hills, noticed some tents in a valley. It was presumed that they were not the same group that had been seen before. As they tried to surprise the camp they were spotted and the Inuit, about 18 of them, fled in their boats. As the soldiers pursued them they fired their guns hoping to alert Captain Yorke's party to the situation. They managed to trap the fleeing Inuit in a creek and as they had no alternative means of escape by sea they were forced to beach their kayaks on the shore. They immediately broke their paddles to render their kayaks useless to their pursuers. Then they turned to fight, firing their bows and arrows with great skill. They were extremely valiant in battle, even pulling arrows, which had been fired by the soldiers, out of their own flesh, and then firing them back again. Their weapons were primitive when compared with those of the soldiers and so the outcome was inevitable. When all hope of victory was lost and they were mortally wounded, they threw themselves off the rocks into the sea and perished. One soldier was wounded in the stomach, five or six Inuit were killed and all the others escaped. Two women were captured, one was released but the other, who was much younger and had an infant with her, was kept. After the skirmish they named the place "Bloody Point" (see map on page 22).

Skirmish at Bloody Point by John White.

When they returned to the tents they found the clothing, letter and other English articles and realised that the Inuit were indeed the same group that Captain Yorke had previously seen. They concluded that the 5 men, captured on the first voyage, must have perished at the hands of this group. This was reinforced by a closer examination of the shirt, which was full of holes, probably made by Inuit darts and arrows. With this sad news, and their captive woman, they returned to the ships in Countess of Warwick Sound and the woman was introduced to her fellow captive. They were kept together and she immediately began to look after the man, but they were never sexually intimate and always hid their private parts from each other and everyone else. She kept their cabin extremely clean and killed and prepared the dogs for eating. He for his part would not even change his clothes without sending the woman out of the cabin.

The danger of reprisals meant that the miners had to be protected and so fortifications were prepared and a guard set. As the miners worked, true to form a group of Inuit appeared on the top of a hill closeby. They were waving a flag and gesticulating and shouting wildly. They had clearly come to complain about their losses and to beg for the release of the man and woman. Martin had the woman displayed on another hilltop and went with the man to confer with them. The man wept uncontrollably as he met with his friends. When he had composed himself, he had a long conversation and gave them some of the toys and gifts that had been given to him. They were very kind to one another and were obviously very upset by the loss of their friends. Martin used sign language to tell them that he would release the prisoners if they returned his five men. They indicated that the men were still alive and they asked Martin to write a letter to them, which they would then take to them. Martin obliged them, in the vain hope that what they said was true. When they had received the letter they left, promising to return in three days.

The letter from Martin read:

"In the name of God, in whom we all believe, who I trust hath preserved your bodies and souls amongst these infidels, I commend me unto you. I will be glad to seek all means you can devise for your deliverance, either with force, or with any commodities within my ships, which I will not spare for your sakes, or anything else I can do for you, but the man which I carried away hence the last year is dead in England. Moreover, you may declare unto them, that if they deliver you not, I will not leave a man alive in their country. And thus, if one of you can come to speak with me, they shall have either the man, the woman, or child in pawn for you. And thus unto God, whom I trust you do serve, in haste I leave you, and to him we will daily pray for you. This Tuesday morning the seventh day of August, Anno 1577.

Yours to the uttermost of my power,

Martin Frobisher

Postscript; I have sent you by these bearers, pen, ink, and paper, to write back unto me again, if personally you can not come to certify me of your estate". [7]

On Saturday 11th August, the Inuit appeared again and Martin crossed the sound to meet them. There were only three of them visible and Martin, suspecting a trap, had stationed some of his men out of sight on high ground so that they could warn him of an ambush. It was a very wise move because they soon spotted many more Inuit creeping amongst the rocks towards Martin. They shouted loudly to warn Martin of the ambush and he quickly withdrew and thus avoided capture or worse. The Inuit then lined up on the hill and displayed their strength. Martin fired his guns to frighten them, rather than to do them any harm, and they ran away. From then on the Inuit tried all manner of methods to capture some of Martin's men but none of their tricks worked. On one occasion they tried to trick them by carrying one of their men to the water's edge. He feigned lameness and they no doubt hoped that Martin's men would take advantage of this and try to capture him, but in the process they would be captured themselves. He was not a very good actor and Martin ordered one of his men to aim a shot at the lame man's legs. His aim was true and the man was hit. His lameness miraculously disappeared and he darted off as fast as he could to hide with his friends behind the rocks. It transpired that over one hundred Inuit were spread out along the shoreline ready to attack Martin and his men. All their efforts were futile and Martin and his men returned safely to the ships.

Meanwhile the miners and their helpers had almost finished their task and had loaded the *Ayde* with about 200 tons of "ore". For twenty days they had laboured together and by the time they had finished they had worn out their clothing and tools. Many of them had been injured and all were weary. With great courage and willingness they had overcome all the difficulties that had arisen and the task was completed on 21st August. By this time the temperature was dropping and ice was forming around the ships at night. The next day they built a large bonfire on the highest hill and marched all round the island, with their English flag flying. They fired a volley of shots in honour of the Right Honourable Lady Anne, Countess of Warwick. Then they set sail for home.

They had a perilous journey as they travelled Southeast. In one severe storm on 30th August the sea was so rough and the waves so mountainous that the master and the boatswain were unfortunately swept overboard. The boatswain was saved but the master, William Smith, perished. When the storm abated the ships had become separated from each other and the raging seas had so pounded the *Ayde* that her rudder had split and was totally ineffective. If it could not be repaired the ship would be helpless and at the mercy of the next storm. It was certain that without steerage she would never get back to England. The crew's survival and indeed their very lives depended on repairing the rudder. A number of men who were good swimmers courageously took it in turns to dive into the freezing sea to effect the necessary repairs. They worked under water, lashing planks to the broken rudder with ropes. When they surfaced and were pulled on board they were gasping for breath, had turned blue with the intense cold and were half-dead. Their heroic efforts however were successful and the ship was able to steer her course and continue on her journey home.

The *Ayde* arrived back in England and anchored at Padstow in Cornwall and then moved to Milford Haven in Wales on 23rd September. They were then ordered to sail to Bristol, which was the second most important port in England at that time. The "ore" was deposited and locked away under Bristol Castle for safe keeping. The *Gabriel* had already arrived at Bristol and the *Michael* was safe in a harbour further north. During the whole voyage they had only lost one person, apart from a sailor who had been ill when he first came aboard and who later died. This was a remarkable achievement of outstanding leadership considering the places they had been to and the perils they had faced. Martin's fame spread far and wide.

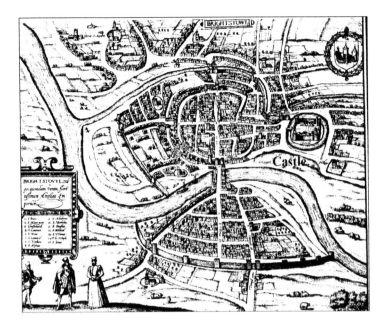

Brightstowe (Bristol) and Castle in the 16th Century.

The site of Bristol Castle today.

After his epic journey Martin went to Windsor Castle to inform Elizabeth of all that had happened on the Second Voyage. He told her of the discoveries he had made and the many dangers and hazards that had been endured. He described the lands and their inhabitants and the possible financial rewards that were to be had in that region. She commended him, the Captains and all the men for their courage and commitment. She appointed experts to assess the outcome of the voyage and to advise her concerning future voyages. She named the newly discovered land "Meta Incognita". The commissioners reported that there were strong reasons for believing that there was indeed a Northwest Passage to Cathay and that gold had been found in the "ore". It was likely that all the costs of further voyages would be more than met by the riches extracted from the "ore" which would be brought back and they strongly recommended that a third voyage warranted royal backing.

It was agreed that it would be advantageous for an experimental settlement to be established in Meta Incognita and a skilful builder was employed to build a sectional portable house to be taken on the next voyage. This would then be fortified, and a group of well-chosen soldiers and practical men would be left to overwinter in the house and thus to care for the mines and to further explore the area. There was no shortage of brave volunteers and it shows that adventurous spirits abounded in Elizabethan England, but no doubt they were helped along by the promise of gold. They would have to face all the truly terrible weather conditions of the arctic winter with its intense cold, blizzards, ice and storms; also the bare terrain and the fierce local inhabitants. Sailors, miners, soldiers, bakers, carpenters, tradesmen and gentlemen, were all chosen for this ambitious and rather foolhardy project.

All preparations were completed for the Third Voyage and

fifteen ships were assembled at Harwich in Essex on the East Coast. It was the largest expedition ever to brave the arctic seas. Before departing, the fifteen captains went to Greenwich to bid farewell to their Queen. She received them well and graciously encouraged them, promising them rich rewards if the voyage had a successful outcome. She gave Martin a golden chain. He kissed her hand, as did the other captains, and they returned to Harwich to join their ships.

Erratum page 45   List of ships
The Ayde   Captain Frobisher
The Thomas Allen   Captain Yorke
The Judith   Captain Fenton
The Anne Frances   Captain Best etc

CHAPTER 5

THE THIRD ARCTIC VOYAGE—1578

On May 27[th,] 1578 Martin, as General of the voyage, gathered his captains together and gave them their written orders and articles. There were fifteen orders in all, the first one being "To banish swearing, dice, card playing, and filthy communication; and to serve God twice daily with the ordinary service of the Church of England, and to clear the glass according to the old order in England".[8] Martin took the Christian faith very seriously and expected it to be practised aboard all his ships. It meant that morale, discipline and good order were maintained by everyone on the expedition.

The 15 ships and their captains were: -

The Ark	Captain Frobisher
The Thomas Allen	" Yule
The Anne Frances	" Fenton
The Hopewell	" Carew
The Bear	" Filpot
The Thomas of Ipswich	" Tanfield
The Emmanuel of Exeter	" Courtney
The Frances of Foy	" Moyles
The Moon	" Upcot
The Emma of Bridgewater	" Newton
The Salmon of Weymouth	" Randall
The Dennis	" Kendall
The Gabriel	" Harvey
The Michael	" Kinnersley

The ships set sail on May 31st and followed the south coast of England along the Channel and then Northwest towards Ireland. On their way they met a ship in distress. She was from Bristol and had been attacked by a French vessel. During the battle for control of the ship many of the crew had been killed and others badly wounded. Their situation was desperate for they had completely run out of supplies and if Martin had not stopped to help they would certainly have perished. However, with the help and supplies that Martin had given them, they managed to limp home to port. The fleet then proceeded northwards along the West Coast of Ireland and found themselves in a very strong current. To compensate for the current which was running from Southwest to Northeast they had to make constant adjustments to their navigation as they sailed North and West (this current would be what we now call the Gulf Stream). After sailing for two weeks they landed on West Friesland (probably the south of Greenland) which they presumed was an island and Martin took possession of it for Elizabeth. They explored the area briefly and investigated some tents they came across and concluded that they belonged to people who were very similar to those living in Meta Incognita. Some even believed the land was part of Meta Incognita and others that it was Greenland and not an island at all.

On 23rd June they set sail for Meta Incognita and sailed into a large school of whales. The *Salmon* struck one of the huge monsters so square on that the ship was stopped dead in her tracks. The whale shuddered and emitted a loud and most fearsome noise and then dived. Later they found a dead whale floating on the surface and presumed it to be the same one that had collided with the *Salmon.* After passing through large quantities of ice they finally arrived in Frobisher's Straits. To their great disappointment the straits were packed almost solid with ice.

This presented the ships' captains with a tricky problem for the ice was moving and heaving all around them, pressing in on their hulls. Manoeuvring about was extremely dangerous. One ship would follow another into a clear passage of water and then quite suddenly the ice would move and quickly close in on them. It was extremely difficult to avoid being crushed because they were reliant on wind power and tacking was almost impossible among the ice. Two ships, the *Judith* and the *Michael* had already gone missing. The *Dennis* (100 tons) was holed below the waterline so badly by the ice that she sank. Fortunately the endangered crew had time to fire their ordnance before the ship sank and they thus attracted the attention of other ships which were nearby. They immediately responded and all the crew was rescued. Unfortunately, part of the portable house was on board the *Dennis* and was lost with the ship.

Having witnessed the demise of the *Dennis* they were suddenly struck by a most fearsome arctic storm. The gale force winds from the Southeast forced the pack ice into the mouth of the straits and the flotilla of ships was trapped and totally cut off from the open sea. As the ice threatened them from every side, it was every ship for herself. The crews, using their ingenuity, had to try all sorts of ways and means to defend their ships from the raging storm and the ice. Some found a small patch of clear water and furled their sails and then drifted. Others tied up to large icebergs on the side away from the wind and thus were somewhat protected. Others became trapped between gigantic slabs of ice and had to wait almost helplessly until a sudden movement in the sea below released the ship from the deadly grip of the ice. The men did everything they could think of to protect the hulls of their ships. They used cables, beds, masts, planks and anything else they could find to hang over the side to ease the pressure on the hull. Some men even risked their lives by jumping out of their ships and going on to the ice where they used pikes, poles, pieces of timber and oars to fend off the slabs of ice. They worked in such extremely cold and appalling weather conditions that it was nothing short of a miracle that they were able to continue for as long as they did. Day and night they toiled, their captains encouraging them and urging them on. There is no doubt that it was only the Herculean efforts of the crews that saved most of the ships from being crushed and destroyed during that storm. The ice was so powerful that it was able to slice through three inch thick planks and whole ships were lifted a foot out of the sea.

What sort of men were these? They were men of valiant spirits and big hearts who did not know what it was to give in to the raging elements. As many laboured to save their ships and their lives, others prayed to God for the salvation of their souls and for deliverance from their awful plight. None were idle. All but four of the ships were caught up in the calamity that lasted all day and night and part of the next day. Eventually the storm abated and a favourable wind began to clear the ice from the straits. It was quite remarkable that all the ships survived. The exhausted crews rested their weary bodies, tended their wounds, regained their strength and then set about repairing their bruised ships. George Best wrote of this episode "I dare well avouche, there were never men more daungerouſly diſtreſſed, nor more mercifully by God's Providence delivered". [9]

On July 7th they headed for the straits once more but were carried miles off course by a strong current. They sighted land, which was mistaken for Mount Warwick in Frobisher's Straits. The current was so swift and violent that even these seasoned sailors were amazed by it. The ships were sometimes pivoted around like driftwood in a whirlpool and the sound of the current was like that of the rushing waters as they squeezed through the arches of London Bridge. The truth was that they were completely lost. Martin sent a pinnace to each ship to get the opinions of the other captains. Opinion was so divided that it was of little use. Christopher Hall, the chief pilot, was convinced that he had not seen the coastline before and therefore they could not be in Frobisher's Straits. To make matters even worse the fleet was scattered as they sailed through dense fog, which made it impossible to stay in sight of each other. Martin led the ships that had managed to stay with him further and further into these "Mistaken Straits", which later were to become known as "Hudson Straits". He later confessed that if he had not been responsible for the other ships, he would have sailed on. He was convinced that this might well be the passage that he had yearned to find for so long, and which would lead him to Cathay and the riches of the East.

As they travelled further west the land appeared greener and they noticed that there were more wild animals including some deer. They also sighted more native people and one of the gentlemen on board managed to trade some merchandise with them. They also saw many larger boats belonging to these people that held about twenty people. Martin, while sorely tempted to sail on, allowed his better judgement to prevail and he turned east. With the other ships following he retraced his course. It was a very wise decision for if he had not done so, he and all the others would surely have perished if they had been caught in the grim winter of Hudson Bay. Knowing that Frobisher's Straits must be to the north of them, Martin sent the *Gabriel* to explore a distant sound to see where it went. It led into Frobisher's Straits and thus proved that the Queen's Foreland was an island. Martin then led the fleet through the sound into Frobisher's Straits amid much rejoicing. Once there they sailed into another dense fog, which was bad enough, but an extremely strong current further compounded their problems. As there was very little wind at the time the ships could not make any headway and were therefore carried along helplessly by the current which all the while carried the ships toward the shore. Sometimes they passed over rocks beneath them with barely a foot to spare. Many times as they drifted out of control they were convinced that they would be wrecked on reefs and rocks along the shoreline but then a sudden freshening of the wind would come to the rescue and enable them to regain control and manoeuvre out of danger. Frequently they cried out in prayer, "Lorde nowe help or never: nowe Lorde looke downe from Heaven and fave us finners, or elfe oure fafetie commeth too late: even then the mightie maker of Heaven, and oure mercifull God, did deliver us: fo that they who have bin partakers of thefe daungers, do even in their fouls confeffe, that God euen by miracle hath foughte to fave them, whofe name be praifed evermore". [10]

All the ships eventually found their way back and assembled off Hatton's Headland, the southern tip of Queen's Foreland. The *Anne Frances*, separated from the fleet for twenty days, was reunited with them on July 23rd. There was great joy at the reunion and the meeting was accompanied by the usual firing of guns. After hearing about the perils and hardships which the ships and their crews had endured, many of the men became so fearful about their situation and the dangers that they were likely to face that they began to grumble. Some wanted to find a harbour to rest and to care for their damaged ships, others wanted to return home, believing it better to face the hangman's noose than to perish in a storm or the grip of the ice. Martin was resolute in the face of this discontent. He would not allow himself to be diverted from his commission and so he decided to proceed into the Straits. There they would mine and load the "ore" as Queen Elizabeth herself had ordered. If they became trapped and escape became impossible then he would use all the remaining gunpowder to blow up the ships along with their crews, and thus prevent them from falling into the hands of the local inhabitants.

So Martin set off in the *Ayde*, with a pinnace, to look for "ore". Suddenly another howling gale arose and yet again every ship had to fend for herself. During the storm the temperature dropped dramatically and six inches of snow fell and covered the ships. The men were soaked to the skin and suffered terribly from the cold but, despite all the many difficulties, Martin led the *Ayde* through the ice pack in his pinnace, personally pushing the ice floes aside. He cleared a way for the others to follow until at last they arrived in the Countess of Warwick Sound. Having arrived safely it was very unfortunate that a huge slab of ice struck the *Ayde*. It hit her anchor with such force that the fluke of the anchor pierced the hull below the waterline. The ship began to leak so profusely that it took the crew all their time to bail her out and stop her from sinking.

When they arrived in the Sound they were filled with relief and great joy because to their utter surprise the missing *Gabriel* and *Michael* were anchored there. It had been assumed that they had been lost with all hands and so to celebrate their good fortune there were the usual celebrations and firing of guns. Mr Wolfall, the fleet's minister, led the men in prayers of thanksgiving and preached a fine sermon. He reminded them of their miraculous deliverance and the uncertainties of life. Mr Wolfall was a prosperous man and had a wife and family back in England. He had volunteered to go on the voyage because he longed to reach the Inuit peoples with the Christian gospel and thus to save their souls. He was a very godly man and was even willing to give up his own life while ministering to his flock on the voyage. He desperately wanted to be chosen to stay for the overwintering experiment in Meta Incognita so that he could meet and minister to the Inuit people.

The crews of the *Gabriel* and *Michael* recited the dangers that they had experienced while separated from the fleet. They had been trapped in the ice for twenty days and the ships had been crushed and pierced by icebergs and only Providence and their ingenuity had saved them. One huge iceberg was measured and found to be nearly four hundred feet high. It amazed them when they realised that the bulk of the iceberg was below the water. They were also surprised to discover that when the sun melted the ice on the surface, it was not salty, and ran down the icebergs in small brooks, with sufficient power to drive a waterwheel at a mill. After listening to their stories Martin called a meeting of his council to plan their next strategy. Leaders were appointed and orders were drawn up and on August 1st all the captains were given the orders and the mining and loading of "ore" was to commence. The next day a blast on a trumpet called the whole company together. Instructions for their stay were published, "Orders set down by M. Frobisher Esquire, Captain General for the voyage to Cathay, to be observed of the company, during the time of their abode in Meta Incognita".[11]

The orders included:

A ban on trading or fighting with the Inuit,
A prohibition on keeping any precious stone or metal for oneself
All ore to be checked officially before loading
A ban on swearing, brawling and cursing
A ban on using weapons in a quarrelsome manner
Preserving the purity of their fresh water supply and arrangements for toilets.

No litter or rubbish to be thrown from the ships but disposed of safely.

While the miners began their work the captains went off to find other rich deposits of "ore". The work was somewhat hindered because the four missing ships had some of the best miners on board and also some of the materials for building the house. Captain Fenton, with sixty volunteers, had offered to stay during the winter months and would await the return of a further voyage the next year. They chose Kodlunarn Island in Countess of Warwick Sound (see map on page 34) as their base and where the house would be built and their supplies stored. The craftsmen estimated that it would take at least nine weeks to build the house because as already mentioned half of it had been lost in the *Dennis* when she foundered. In any case it could only be done if they could find sufficient timber. They did not see how this was to be achieved because there were only four weeks left before the fleet had to leave for England and there was no wood to be found anywhere. When the council met and considered these matters, and that on top of everything else there were insufficient supplies for over-wintering, it was regretfully agreed to abandon the project. It was clearly not a feasible proposition and no doubt those involved in the overwintering would have perished if the plan had proceeded. They built a smaller version of the house and the island still retains its ruins.

The four ships which were still missing, (the *Anne Frances, Moon, Thomas of Ipswich* and *Thomas Allen*) also went through many dangerous episodes as they tried to find and rejoin the fleet. The weather as usual was appalling, with high winds opposing their progress and the ice being a constant hazard. The *Moon* at one point was severely damaged as it was alarmingly squeezed and lifted out of the water. The exhausted crews fought magnificently against wind, sea and ice. The ships were leaking badly and the sailors' hands were lacerated through handling the icy ropes and rigging. Many of the men became discouraged and favoured returning to England. After all they didn't know whether the other ships had foundered or not. Even if they hadn't, they might continue to search for them and still not find them. The captains loyal to the cause overruled them and decided to go on.

Captain Tanfield of the *Thomas of Ipswich* and a band of men took the pinnace from the *Moon* and found an island that was rich in the "ore". After returning with the good news the ships made sail and went to the island. Although they sounded the channel very carefully the *Anne Frances* sailed on to a submerged rock and was unable to extricate herself. Very fortunately, and much to the men's relief, she was refloated on the next tide and the damage she sustained was repaired. Meanwhile the miners got to work and began to mine the "ore" ready for loading. The captains got the carpenters to prepare a pinnace for a lengthy journey so that a party could go in search of Martin and the rest of the fleet. Captain Best of the *Anne Frances*, Captain Upcot of the *Moon* and eighteen men set off and were successful in finding the fleet on August 23rd. There were jubilant celebrations again. Martin was absolutely delighted because he had feared the worst. After the celebrations were over he called a meeting of all the captains and aboard the *Ayde* they discussed the possibility of a further voyage in 1579.

On the 24th August, Martin and Captain Best set out with three pinnaces to see if they could capture some of the local Inuit who they were still convinced were cannibals. The Inuit were far too suspicious and elusive and avoided all their efforts. The only thing they managed to take back with them was a large Inuit dart that was left behind in their forsaken camp. Later that night Captain Best walked overland via Hatton's' Headland to find his ship the *Anne Frances.* His men were delighted to see him and to hear the news that he had found the rest of the fleet. They had already worked hard and had loaded the ship with "ore" and were ready to sail. The next morning, August 30th, the *Anne Frances* rejoined the fleet and the eight large leaks in her hull were repaired. Meanwhile Captain Fenton and his men had finished building the house on Kodlunarn Island, but it had to be much smaller than the original design. The idea was to inspect it when they returned on the next voyage to see how it had faired during the arctic winter. Many other items including victuals were either buried nearby or stored in the house.

It was on this occasion that the Chaplain, Mr Wolfall, organised a service, preached a fine sermon and celebrated the Communion Service according to the Book of Common Prayer of the Church of England. This was the first occasion that this service was conducted on the American Continent. Afterwards Martin held another meeting with the Captains and Gentlemen because he was still determined to search for the Northwest Passage. He felt that the foray into the Mistaken Straits was not enough and he wanted to extend his knowledge of that area. The meeting decided that it was too dangerous to delay their return journey but it was agreed that Martin should take a pinnace for a while and explore further northwards. A date was set for him to return which gave time for the ships to be loaded with "ore" and to be made ready for the return voyage. This was the last time that Martin went in search of the Northwest Passage. He reached as far as Bear's Sound and Hall's Island but was very disappointed to find that the land was broken up into lots of small islands and his search was over. He had however sailed into the unknown and charted the area and had discovered and claimed new lands for Elizabeth which all brought him great fame. He returned to the fleet and gave instructions for the return voyage:

> All the ships were to keep together with the Admiral.
> All instructions to be applied to every ship
> No person shall have any of the "ore" for themselves
> No "ore" or any other articles to be taken off any ship until off loaded at Dartford Creek in the River Thames
> Any items received by anyone on the voyage to be handed to their Captain and then to the Admiral.
> If a ship becomes separated from the fleet due to bad weather and then is in danger of being captured they shall throw overboard all maps, charts and references to the newly discovered lands
> Any ship that becomes separated and arrives at an English port shall immediately notify Michael Lok and not leave the port
> All tools and implements used on the voyage to be handed over to the Admiral so that they can be returned to the miners and craftsmen.

All these Articles were accompanied with punishments for those who disobeyed them.

The return voyage began almost disastrously on August 31st 1578. They were about to leave when a ferocious storm arose and struck the fleet. At the same time the *Judith* and the *Anne Frances* were still taking on fresh water from the shore. The storm struck with such force that the men ashore could not return to the ships in the pinnaces because of the heavy surf whipped up by the gale. Martin and some of his men bravely left the ships to collect the marooned men on the shore. Meanwhile, the ships offshore were in danger of being blown on to the rocks along the coast and were being severely threatened by large slabs of ice, which they knew from experience could easily pierce their hulls. As the storm eased somewhat the men were all rescued but Martin had to board the *Gabriel,* a much smaller ship than the *Ayde* and able to approach closer to the shore. They immediately set sail for England, no doubt very relieved to be leaving a place where they had met with so many perils. The fleet by now had been well and truly scattered by the storm. Twenty small boats and pinnaces had been lost in the storm and some men had been washed overboard and drowned. Battered and separated from each other, the ships sailed back to England as best they could and docked in various ports on or about the 5th October 1578. George Best's final words in his account show how truly successful the voyage had been, "There dyed in the whole Fleete in all the voyage not above fortie perfons, whiche number is not great, confidering howe many fhips were in the Fleete, and how ftrange Fortunes wee paffed".[12] It is interesting to note that when ships returned to port after extensive voyages, the local authorities were very cautious, and took steps to prevent the spread of diseases. Martin was ordered to keep all his ships' companies on board until their Lordships gave permission for them to disembark. Likewise he was forbidden to allow London's inhabitants to go aboard in case they spread the plague or other diseases to the crews and visa versa. "On return from his third voyage to the North West Martin Frobisher was ordered that by reason of plague he permit no inhabitant of London or places thereabouts to board his ships, nor to suffer any of his crews to go ashore till he shall be otherwise advised by their Lordships".[13]

The third voyage had been a huge combined enterprise of discovery, mining of "ore", and transporting it back to England. It was an amazing feat of leadership, courage, skill and endurance. After the expedition's return John Kirkham wrote in praise of Martin Frobisher:

> "Earth and skies, the surging seas,
> And Sylvane Echoes brave,
> Do all resound with tuned string
> Of silver harmony
> How Frobisher, in every coast,
> With flickering fame doth fly
> A Martial Knight, adventurous,
> Whose valour great was such
> That hazards hard he light esteemed
> His country to enrich". [14]

CHAPTER 6

"ALL THAT GLITTERS!"

After the return from Meta Incognita in 1578 things looked very promising indeed. Martin had brought home safely most of the ships and their crews. They had endured and overcome intense cold, fog, ice and numerous ferocious storms. They had deposited hundreds of tons of "ore" at Dartford on the Thames. He had led the expedition with great skill and discipline and had claimed new lands for Elizabeth. On the other hand, he had been diverted from his first priority—to discover the Northwest Passage. The nagging question of whether there was gold in the "ore" remained unsolved. Michael Lok had invested very heavily in the project, as had many others, but to date no gold of any quantity had been refined. The following letter implies that gold had indeed been found in the "ore" and that much more was to follow:

> "21st February 1577, from D Burcotte, with a Proof how much gold and silver a pound, and one Hundredth Pound weight which he will warrant to hould throughout the whole Ore.
> Please your honour, I perceive by your letter that you cannot come so quickly as I thought, therefore, I send you here by the captain the silver and gold of a pound, and a hundred weight, where by I will abide by it off my credit and honesty that I will bringe twenty times

so much out of every ton in the like loss much this Spring to go about that business; and that you will be ameane that the captain may be speedily set forth again with such teaching and instruction, as I have given him, for if he shall not go speedily and specially now this year it will be the worst that ever came to England, and that the ore may be brought hastily from Bristol to Dartford and that the detymente that the captain can show you be prepared, and your Honour to come so hastily as you can to visit the place where the melting house shall stand. Now I send you the truth by the captain how the house shall be; and I trust to see you shortly. So I commit your Honour to God in haste, this 21st day of February, 1578.

Your Honour to command

Burchard Kraurych

To his honourable and singular friend, Sir Francis Walsingham

Secretary to the Queens Highness, deliver this". [15]

While many records show that the "ore" did not contain gold others show that gold had been smelted from it:

"Baptista and Jonas made divers other proofs thereof whereby still they found gold which afterwards was discovered to Sir William Winter by Sir William Morgan.

In the beginning of April 1577, when Sir William Winter was assured from Sir William Morgan and Sir John Bartley, by the handiwork of Jonas, by proofs which he made in their own presence, to their own satisfaction that this was truly the ore of a mine of

gold; the said Sir William Winter justified the same to
be true to my Lords of the Queen's Majesties Honourable Privy Council".[16]

The furnaces at Sir William Winter's house, Dartford were
built by Jonas and were completed just before Martin's return.
By the 30th October Jonas had said that he had found that a ton
of ore produced more fine gold of greater value than was first
thought. The problem was that no actual gold of any quantity
had been forthcoming and the merchants and the Queen's authorities were getting more concerned. All sorts of schemes and
methods to extract the gold were considered and tried. Indeed
in those days of primitive smelting it could well be the case that
any gold, which had appeared at the end of the process, had come
from other ingredients used in the process rather than from the
"ore" itself. It is clear that the allure of gold, so dominant in
people's thinking, and the poor smelting techniques, led to the
final outcome that the "ore" was not "ore" at all. It was just rock
and nothing more. Consequently many disillusioned investors
who could now only lose their money didn't honour their com-
mitments. Inevitably the Company collapsed with large debts
and with wages unpaid. Martin's wife Isabella had not been well
cared for and resided in a poor house. Recriminations, charges
and counter charges were furiously exchanged and many were
humiliated as well as losing a lot of money. Lok stood to lose
the most. The 3 voyages and associated activities cost £20,160
and Lok had invested £4,920. Poor Michael Lok finished up in
jail as a bankrupt. Martin like many others lost money but he
also lost his patience and was furious with the smelters, who
had always promised so much, but in the end delivered virtually nothing. All parties, along with many before them and no
doubt many to come, learned the truism that "All that glitters

is not gold". We now know that the black rock was calc-silicate gneiss, and the reddish rock was metasandstone. The flecks of "gold" which sparkled, and which were to be seen in the rocks on the beaches in that area, were flecks of biotite mica. And so the rock, brought back from Baffin Island at such great risk, cost and hard labour proved to be just that. It was eventually used for building walls and repairing roads and remnants of the rock can still be seen in the walls of a ruined manor house at Dartford in Southeast London.

Rocks from Kodlunarn Island Area brought back to England by George Frobisher in 1980.

Martin however does not seem to have lost his reputation. After all, he had led a very large and dangerous expedition very successfully and his leadership and seamanship were proven beyond question. The three voyages had added significantly to what was known about the Arctic region. It had also increased the pool of nautical expertise that English seamen were steadily acquiring and from which they would benefit in the future. There are those who have argued that Martin and others knew full well, before the 1578 voyage, that the rock was worthless. This does not really stand up to scrutiny. Men would surely not venture their very lives and substantial monies in extremely dangerous seas for something they knew to be worthless. The most likely explanation is that the assayers, who said that the rock contained gold, were believed rather than those who said it did not. While the rock yielded no gold, the search for the Northwest Passage, the exploration of the region, the claim of lands for England and the contact with the indigenous people were greatly admired. It was left to Davis, between 1585 and 1587, to follow in Sir Martin's footsteps as he ventured forth to make further discoveries in the Northwest.

In 1994 a group of Archaeologists from Laval University, Quebec visited Kodlunarn Island in Countess of Warwick Sound and found the island to be a unique two-year time capsule of Frobisher's activities. Charles Hall had previously landed on the island in 1861. He had heard from the Inuit of that area tales about some white men who had visited the region many years earlier. He realised they could only be referring to Frobisher's voyages. Dr Walter Kenyon who led the 1994 expedition found various excavations on the island, one of which could have been used as a mine or for the repairing of ships and another one as a mine or reservoir. Items were well preserved and the foundations of the house were still intact. Remains of a primitive blacksmith's shop were also discovered. There was evidence that it contained a furnace that must have been used to heat the "ore". Fragments of crucibles and refractory ceramics were found and some had glassy surfaces which indicate that they had been heated to high temperatures. The researchers have concluded that this must be the earliest industrial enterprise in the New World undertaken by the English. Previously it had been claimed that the laboratory at Sir Walter Raleigh's Roanoak Colony in Virginia, set up in 1585/86 had been first. Martin's laboratory and associated industrial activities carried out on Kodlunarn Island between 1576 and 1578 were ten years earlier.

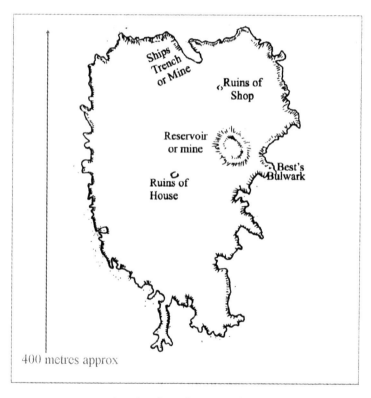

Sketch of Kodlunarn Island.

CHAPTER 7

WITH DRAKE TO THE SPANISH MAIN

Early in 1579 Martin was called upon by the Privy Council to command the Queen's ship *Foresight*. His mission was to take the protestant Duke John Casimir and his troops across the English Channel to Flushing. It must have been a pleasant diversion from all the troubles associated with the smelting at Dartford. When this task was successfully completed he looked for further employment. He had previously been involved in the pacification of Ireland and the Queen and her advisers were still concerned about the threat from Catholic Ireland, which was growing. Rebellion was in the air. Martin was ordered to join Sir William Winter's fleet and he took command of the *Foresight* again. His role was to transport soldiers and supplies from England to Ireland in aid of the Queen's land army. Martin's experience at sea had taught him that an expedition was only as successful as their victuals allowed. Many ships and their crews were sent on their missions without adequate provisions. This was common amongst the English ships and it caused hunger, disease and death amongst the crews and thereby inhibited their effectiveness. He dared to point this out to the Privy Council: "If the allowance be not full and the victual good, it is not possible to prolong the time of service beyond the proportion of victual; but if her Majesty's allowance be full, and the victual good, it may be drawn to some longer time upon an extremity". [17] After he had completed the work in Ireland he petitioned the Queen for further gainful employment. She granted his request and he took the position of Clerk of the Ships. However, he was a man of action and not the sort of man to hold an administrative position for long. He probably sold the lease for the position soon afterwards.

Little is known of Martin's activities during 1581. Some think he returned to privateering in order to generate an income. Whatever else he did, we know that by 1582 he had been chosen to command a small fleet to trade with the Portuguese. He was well advanced with preparations for this voyage when it was decided to replace him. This decision was probably made because the merchant backers remembered the disastrous financial outcome of the 1578 Northwest voyage. Edward Fenton was chosen to replace him and the fleet set sail in 1582. It wasn't long before there was an outbreak of indiscipline and unruly behaviour amongst the crews and the voyage ended in complete disaster. Fenton had not been able to maintain discipline amongst the ships' companies. The replacement of Martin must have been deeply regretted because he would undoubtedly have dealt with any breakdown in discipline, if it had been allowed to develop at all, and he would have surely returned home with handsome profits. It did his reputation no harm at all so much so that he was soon appointed as an advisor to the Privy Council commissioners.

By 1585 the political world was heading for a crisis. Spain had annexed Portugal after the death of King Henry and she was therefore more powerful than ever. England was challenging Spain for supremacy at sea and was exploring the New World across the Atlantic. Gilbert for example had founded colonies in America. Raleigh had also established colonies in Virginia.

The tension between Elizabeth of England and Philip of Spain, between Protestant and Catholic States intensified. Philip ordered an embargo to be put on all English ships and goods in all his dominions. Elizabeth responded by authorising English ships to capture Spanish vessels and take their cargoes as booty. This was meat and drink to those like Frobisher who had already gained expertise in such matters. In this political climate two major expeditions were authorised. Bernard Drake was instructed to take a fleet to Newfoundland to plunder the Spanish fishing industry and to bring the fish back into West Country ports. Francis Drake was at the same time assembling a powerful expedition to go to the Far East. Instead he was instructed to organise and take command of a large fleet of 25 ships, manned by 2300 men. Martin was appointed as his vice admiral and was therefore second in command. It was the largest fleet that had ever crossed the Atlantic. They were ordered to sail to the Spanish Main to plunder Spanish wealth.

They left Plymouth on 12th September 1585 and sailed south for Spain. Off the coast they came across some French ships and Martin, in his flagship *Primrose*, went with some pinnaces to ascertain what they were and what business they were on. As they approached the French ships, their crews fled ashore. Martin and his men boarded the ships and found that they were returning to France with cargoes of salt. Martin brought the *Madaleine*, the best of the French ships to Drake, and he liked it so much that he commandeered it and promised to pay for it when he returned to England (which promise he kept). They named the "borrowed" vessel *Drake*. The remaining eight ships were left without anything being taken from them. This showed that some honour was still maintained and that the Englishmen's argument at that time was with Spain and not with France. The same courtesy was afforded to another French fleet returning to

France from Newfoundland with cargoes of fish. Not so lucky however was a Spanish ship full of dried fish. She was taken as a prize and her dried fish was distributed amongst the English ships, which proved to be a very welcome and tasty addition to their crew's menu for many weeks to come.

They arrived at the mouth of the River Vigo and because of a lack of wind Drake and all the men able to fit in the pinnaces, rowed ashore. As they approached the City of Bayon an English merchant met them. He had been sent by the city's Governor to see who they were and what they wanted. Drake sent Captain Sampson with the merchant to put two questions to the Governor: did he know of any wars between Spain and England and why were English merchants being arrested and their goods put under an embargo? Captain Sampson returned and reported that the Governor knew nothing about a war with England and that the embargo had been lifted seven days previously. So the city averted violence and the Governor sent welcome refreshments for Drake's men. About midnight any further involvement with Bayon was suddenly concluded. A violent storm arose and the ships, which were at anchor, were being severely battered and some had already dragged their anchors. The *Speedwell* was unable to recover her position and had to return to England. The storm lasted a full three days, after which the whole fleet moved to a more sheltered harbour where the men could recover and fresh water could be taken aboard. The Governor of the area, known as Galicia, raised a defensive army of about 2000 foot soldiers and 300 cavalry and they took their defensive stand in sight of the fleet. Martin was sent in a skiff (a small rowing boat) to meet and bring the Governor away from the shore. Drake met him in his skiff, away from the land as a precaution, so that no harm could be done to him or his men. They agreed terms and the fleet was allowed to take on water and other provisions which Drake dutifully paid for. When all this was completed they sailed for the Canary Islands. They intended to land at Palma but this proved impossible because there was only one safe landing place close to the city and this was well defended with cannon. Just how well it was defended very quickly became apparent, because the defenders suddenly opened fire and many ships were hit. Fortunately the damage they sustained was only superficial. They quickly moved on to the Island of Ferro, the most westward of the Canaries. Here they put ashore a thousand men but found the inhabitants so impoverished that they left without doing them any harm. They then set a Southeasterly course and headed for the Barbary Coast of Northwest Africa, a place that Martin knew well from previous voyages. They followed the coast and then turned west for the Cape Verde islands and arrived at the Island of Santiago on the 16th November 1585.

A land army of one thousand men, under Lieutenant-General Christopher Carlile, was put ashore and marched toward the city of Santiago. The next day the city was taken with very little resistance, and the flag of St George was raised so that the fleet anchored offshore could see it. All the ordnance in the town was discharged in honour of the Queen's Coronation Day and the ships responded in kind. No doubt Martin's shipmates were jubilant. Captain Biggs recorded that it was strange to hear such a thundering noise lasting so long. The army was billeted for fourteen days and the ships replenished with supplies and fresh water. No treasure was discovered in the city so Drake ordered the army to return to their respective ships using the pinnaces. Martin stayed behind in the Town Square so that he could bring aboard the last one hundred men who had been stationed to guard the departure of the rest. After leaving Santiago, Drake called at Playa, which was nearby. This town had dealt treacherously with William Hawkins a few years previously and many of his men had been murdered. They had also very foolishly killed one of Drake's men who had wandered off on his own. Not content with just killing him they had brutalised his body and then scattered his body parts. By the time Drake arrived at the city all the people had fled, fearing Drake's revenge. Drake left a written explanation as to why the town was burnt to the ground.

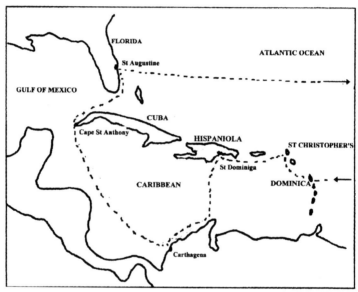

Map of the Spanish Main showing the route of Drake's voyage.

As yet Drake had unwisely not had the men swear the usual oath of allegiance to the Queen and to himself as their Commander. This was done but Captain Francis Knollis was willing to swear an oath of allegiance to the Queen but not to Sir Francis. Martin and the other captains did their very best to persuade him to do so but he wouldn't change his mind and so Drake stripped him of his rank but took no further action. They then left the Verde Islands to cross the Atlantic and set a course for the West Indies and the Spanish Main. A few days into the crossing a deadly infection hit the crews and many men died. Martin lost at least sixty of his men on the *Primrose.* Those who recovered were left in an extremely weakened state and so they were all very relieved, after eighteen days, to come upon the Island of Dominica. The inhabitants there treated them very kindly and carried water, food and tobacco to the ships. As recompense they were given glass, coloured beads and other materials taken from Santiago. They sailed on to the Northwest and celebrated Christmas on an Island called St Christopher's. Here they rested, recovered from their sickness and cleaned and repaired the ships. Drake met with Martin and the other Captains and they decided to sail to the famed city of St. Domingo on the Island of Hispaniola.

On the way to Hispaniola, Martin captured a small frigate that was also bound for St. Domingo. He found out from one of the crew that the city was so well situated and defended that it was almost impossible to attack it from the sea. Therefore the whole army was put ashore about ten miles from the city so that they could march to it and attack from the land. After attacking on two flanks, the city was captured and later that same night, the castle, which guarded the seaward side, was also overrun and taken. They then set up their own defences and held the city for a month. While attacking the city an incident took place which infuriated General Christopher Carlile. He sent a young black boy under a white flag of truce with a message to some Spaniards. They had come from a Spanish galleon that was in the harbour and which was later captured with the city. The boy was brutally attacked and fatally wounded. He died in the General's presence after telling him how he had been cruelly treated. The general ordered two prisoners, who happened to be Friars, to be taken to the spot where the boy was attacked and in full view of the Spaniards they were both hung as a reprisal. The Spaniards were then told to hand over the main perpetrator of the attack on the boy or there would be further hangings. The next day the offender was produced and the General made the Spanish execute him themselves.

Negotiations began for a ransom payment to spare the city. Each morning houses on the outskirts were burnt to press home the best deal. They eventually settled for 25,000 ducats and were surprised that the city was not as wealthy as they had thought. The reason for this was that all the wealth from the gold and silver mines had already been transported to Spain to fill Philip's coffers. The indigenous people were under a severe military tyranny and they didn't benefit at all from the wealth their labours had wrought. This was further reinforced by Captain Biggs' description of a large painting in the Governor's house. The painting hung in a very prominent position so that all who entered the house were bound to view it. It bore the Arms of the King of Spain, with a globe of the world beneath and a horse in a leaping pose. In its mouth was a scroll inscribed with a Latin slogan "NON SUFFICIT ORBIS" (The world is not sufficient). Such aspirations of world dominion, and the power and wealth that would accompany it did not amuse the English. It served to reinforce their view that the Spanish were a real threat to Queen Elizabeth's realm and to England's influence.

Leaving St. Domingo they sailed south to the mainland of South America and then along the coast to Carthagena (the modern town called Cartagena on the northern coast of Columbia). They landed the army that was under Carlile's command. About a hundred horsemen met them but they turned and fled as soon as they came under fire. Martin, with a flotilla of pinnaces and small boats, began a barrage against the fort defending the harbour. This attack could not succeed because the harbour entrance was very narrow and was chained to prevent ships from entering. Martin was merely opening another front by attacking from the sea to divert some of the city's defenders and so make it easier for the land army. Martin was not one to lead from the rear and he was in the forefront of the assault. Cannon shot rained down on them and Martin's pinnace was hit by a saker shot (a three and half inch bore gun with a five pound shot). The shot smashed the rudder but no other harm was done. Meanwhile the land army approached the city during the night from the other direction. They had to overcome very strong defences which consisted of walls with large cannon, demiculverins (four-inch bore, nine pound shot) and sakers. Two galleys in the harbour had been positioned so that they could also fire upon the attackers. These defences, along with small arms, pikes and swords were formidable. It was only by their excellent tactics that the English were able to overcome them. The men crept in silence along the shoreline when the tide was low and then opened fire at a low place in the defences. "Down went the butts of earth, and pell-mell came our swords and pikes together, after our shot had first given their volley, even at the enemy's nose". [18] The attackers had longer pikes and were better armed and the defences were breached very quickly. The Lieutenant General personally killed the Spanish ensign-bearer and the battle was soon over and the city taken. The local Indians fighting alongside the Spaniards fired poisoned arrows at the attacking Englishmen and some were hit and killed. They had also cunningly laid a lot of poisoned spiked sticks in the ground, which were deadly when stepped upon.

They stayed in Carthagena for six weeks and from there they fully intended to move on to Panama to search for greater stores of what had become increasingly elusive Spanish treasure. However the sickness from Santiago was still amongst them and 150 of the men were incapable of strenuous activity, so the leaders met together to decide their next move. They had taken three important Spanish cities which had not yielded as much treasure as expected and it was unlikely therefore that further cities would yield any better. They decided to return to England and accepted 110,000 ducets (which equals about 30,000 pounds sterling) as ransom for Carthagena. This was then shared equally between all the men who had so loyally and at such great sacrifice served in the expedition. After replenishing their supplies and accepting a further ransom of one thousand crowns for an abbey, they left Carthagena on 31st March 1586. Almost immediately after leaving, one of the ships sprang a leak and was in imminent danger of sinking so they had to return to Carthagena. They offloaded the cargo from the stricken vessel and transferred it and the crew into other ships. After a frustrating delay of eight days they set sail north-eastwards for their return voyage. They called at Cape St Anthony on the western tip of Cuba and replenished the ships with fresh water and supplies.

Leaving there on 13th May they sailed northwards along the coast of Florida. On 28th May they spotted a fort on the coast near to St Augustine. It was still under construction and was being built using large tree trunks standing on end. As they approached the fort most of the occupiers took fright and fled inland. They obviously did not want to be around if the large fleet approaching them began a bombardment with their cannon. Suddenly a small boat left the shore and approached the fleet. A lone Frenchman was aboard, all the while playing the song of William of Orange on his fife. He was welcomed with much jocularity and was able to inform them of the nature and defensive strengths of the fort. Drake decided to investigate. He mustered one party and Martin another and in small boats they set off for the fort. Some ordnance was discharged at them but by the time they arrived they found the fort deserted. As they searched it they found a chest containing Spanish treasure worth about two thousand pounds (which presumably they took). They decided that the only reason for the fort being there, and likewise others along the coast was to prevent other nations from taking possession of the land. After destroying the fort and carrying off any valuables they sailed north and on the 9th June spotted a fire on the shore near St Helena. Some English men, who had been left there by Sir Walter Raleigh the year before, had lit the fire to attract the fleet. Delighted that their fire had been seen they were brought aboard, and with their local knowledge piloted the ships into a safe harbour. Drake must have admired these brave settlers who were facing immense difficulties and so he decided to help them by giving them various provisions and one of his ships. They were about to take their leave when the coast was hit by a huge storm of hurricane proportions. It was fortunate indeed that the fleet was in a reasonably sheltered harbour but nevertheless it was severely battered for three days and many of the pinnaces and smaller boats were lost. The storm was so fierce and so unusually savage that it changed the opinion of the settlers and they all decided it was folly to stay and asked for passage to return to England with the fleet. This was granted and they left on 18th June, crossed the Atlantic and arrived at Portsmouth on 28th July 1586. They were hailed as conquering heroes and returned with sixty thousand pounds sterling and all sorts of valuables, including ordnance. During the voyage they had lost 750 men, three quarters of them through sickness. While the expedition had not realised its full financial expectations, the fame of Drake and Frobisher spread throughout the Land. The ego and power of Spain had been seriously challenged by the expedition. After the demands of such a long spell at sea Martin took the opportunity to go home to Altofts in Yorkshire where he used his new wealth to acquire lands and property. His family already owned property and lands around Altofts but he bought a farm for himself in 1586 and by the time of his death in 1594 he possessed extensive estates in the area as well as his farm as follows:

> 1591 He purchased two messuages (a dwelling house with outbuildings and lands) with lands in Heathe, Warmfield and Kirkthorpe. He also bought six messuages and four cottages with all their lands at Warmfield, Kirkthorpe and Normanton.
> 1591/2 He bought from the Queen through Lord Burghley and John Fortesque the Manor of Whitwood and twenty messuages and ten mills with all their lands. Whitwood Manor still stands and is a dwelling house to this day. He bought Finningley Grange, Nottinghamshire for £948. 17s. 3 & 1/2d
> 1593 He bought two messuages with their lands at Brockholes, Brampton and Cantley.

At some point he also built his own manor house on land at Altofts and named it Frobisher Hall. It was demolished in 1859 but one can still see evidence of its foundations in the garden of a modern bungalow.

Whitwood Manor, near Normanton, Yorkshire.

Site of Frobisher Hall, Altofts. Demolished 1859

CHAPTER 8

DEFEAT OF THE SPANISH ARMADA

By 1586 the political enmity between Philip 2nd of Spain and Elizabeth of England had come to a head and Philip ordered the Marquis of Santa Cruz and the Duke of Parma to invade England. Santa Cruz was instructed to prepare a fleet for an invasion from the sea, and Parma was to assemble a land army in the Low Countries to meet up with the fleet. Together they were to land in England and march on London. He hoped that all preparations could be made for the invasion to take place in the autumn of 1587. This proved impossible and it was not until the next Spring that the invasion forces were ready. In the meantime Santa Cruz died on 9th February 1588. This was a major setback, because Santa Cruz was a formidable, able and very experienced commander, who had overseen the plans and preparations. Philip appointed Medina Sidonia to replace him. Sidonia was a quiet and gracious man, of high social standing, but he had virtually no experience of fighting or of commanding such a huge enterprise. He wrote to Philip "The force is so great, and the undertaking so important, that it would not be right for a person like myself, possessing no experience of sea-faring or of war, to take charge of it…I possess neither aptitude, ability, health or fortune".[19] Philip didn't accept his reasoning and so, unwillingly but graciously and in obedience to his sovereign,

Sidonia took command of the fleet which was already amassing at Lisbon.

Portrait of Philip 2nd of Spain by Alonso Sanchez Coella.

Portrait of Queen Elizabeth 1st of England by John Gower.

Queen Elizabeth, in the meantime, had appointed Lord Howard of Effingham to be in command of the English fleet, which by the end of 1587 had been divided into two groups. About ninety ships were based at Plymouth under the command of Howard and Drake. The other group of about thirty ships was at Dover under the command of Lord Henry Seymour. The first group was strategically placed in the west to defend the south coast and the approaches to the English Channel. The second group was stationed in the east to counter the threat from the Duke of Parma's army across the Channel. The English decided to take the fight to the Spaniards. Drake had already shown how vulnerable the Spanish were when anchored in harbour. His audacious raid on Cadiz of 1587, known as the "Singeing of the

King of Spain's beard" was still fresh in people's minds. Howard wrote "The opinion of Sir Francis Drake, Mr Hawkins, Mr Frobisher and others that be of great judgement and experience is that the surest way to meet with the Spanish fleet is upon their coast, or in any harbour of their own, and there to defeat them".[20] It is clear from this that Martin was held in the highest regard and because of his ability and experience his counsel was sought and valued. Drake's comments to the Queen summed up their thinking, "The advantage of time and place in all martial actions is half a victory, which being lost is irrecoverable".[21] The Queen eventually sanctioned the action and Howard, with Drake as his vice admiral, set off with about ninety ships. It was all to no avail because the weather, unusually stormy that year, turned against them in the Bay of Biscay and they had no choice but to return to Plymouth. As they dropped anchor at Plymouth on 22nd of July the Armada was leaving Corunna in Northwest Spain.

On Friday 29th July, Captain Thomas Fleming in the *Golden Hind* sighted a large fleet of Spanish ships off the Isles of Scilly. He returned to Plymouth with the news and legend has it that he found Drake playing bowls on the Hoe. When told that the Armada had been sighted Sir Francis is reputed to have said, "We have time enough to finish the game and beat the Spaniards too." This account was added to the Armada story at least forty years after the event and has been told and retold to generations of children. In fact it probably never happened but it makes a good story. John Lucas's painting of the legend shows the chief commanders of the English fleet around Sir Francis, who is disregarding the news about the sighting of the Spanish fleet and continues to play his game of bowls. Sir Martin is probably the one at the rear of the picture, whispering to a colleague and obviously very displeased about the delay while the Queen's realm was threatened. The fact is that the fleet could not possibly have left the harbour at that time because the tide was out and the wind was in the wrong direction. The wind changed direction later in the day and the tide turned but there was ample time for Sir Francis to finish his game of bowls before boarding ship.

Seymour Lucas, *The Armada in Sight, 1588*, 1880 (detail) oil on canvas, 126.4 x 182.8 Private collection photograph: Ray Woodbury for Art Gallery of New South Wales, Australia.

Photograph from Plymouth Hoe overlooking Drake's Island and Plymouth Sound.

By dawn of Saturday 30th July (Some date these events mainly in late July: I am following those who date them from 30th July to 12th August) the English ships had warped out of Plymouth Sound. Warping was a method of moving a sailing ship when there was little or no wind and this was often the case when the ship was in the shelter of a harbour. A small rowing boat would go ahead of the ship carrying its anchor. The anchor was then dropped and the ship was hauled towards it. It was a slow laborious process but nonetheless effective and the English ships, once out of harbour made way to intercept the Spanish fleet. As soon as the Spanish ships were sighted from land the local warning beacons were lit and successive beacons on hilltops followed suit in relay all over England until the whole country was alerted to the arrival of the Armada. All that day the Spanish fleet, forming a huge crescent shape of 138 ships with 24,000 men on board, began to enter the English Channel. Meanwhile the English fleet from Plymouth in the west, about ninety in number, very skilfully manoeuvred to gain the advantage of the wind direction, which they never lost and which was to prove so decisive in the battles ahead. This was so very important because the ships as sailing vessels depended solely on wind and oar power and never before had such large fleets been set against each other. The strength and direction of the wind would determine any advantage to be gained from the relative positions and speeds of the opposing ships. Another major factor influencing the outcome of the impending engagements between the two fleets was that John Hawkins had altered the design of many of the English warships. Of the 34 royal ships 22 had been built or rebuilt to his new design during the previous ten years.

Sketch of John Hawkins' new design of a 16th Century English warship.

Sketch of the design of a 16th Century Spanish warship.

The newly designed ships were slimmer and had the fore-castle removed, making them sleeker, faster and more manoeuvrable. Another advantage for the English ships, which was to be so decisive in the subsequent battles, was that their guns were much shorter than the Spanish guns, were easier to load and therefore were able to fire more frequently. This was to be very significant in the close encounters with the enemy. All these factors, along with the English captains' knowledge of local conditions and the fact that the Spanish ships were carrying heavier loads, were all to the advantage of the English. Martin commanded the *Triumph;* the largest ship in the English fleet but built in 1562 to the old design. It was therefore larger, wider, and less manoeuvrable than the ships built to the new design. He must have wondered how his rather cumbersome ship would cope when it was part of a flotilla of ships with such unequal capabilites.

Model of HMS Triumph
in the Ward Room of
HMS Drake, Devonport

Model of HMS Triumph made by apprentices at Devonport naval dockyard, Plymouth.

And so the English fleet, under the command of Lord Howard, closed on the Spanish crescent from the windward side and the battle began as the two fleets approached the Eddistone rock off Plymouth. After some small skirmishes the engagement really started when Drake in the *Revenge*, Frobisher in the *Triumph* and Hawkins in the *Victory* set upon the rear of the Crescent. They had previously devised a new method of naval warfare and it took the enemy completely by surprise. They did not try, as was customary, to grapple with and then to board an enemy ship to fight it out on its decks (hence the idea of castles fore and aft to give advantage to the defenders). Instead they approached the enemy but then stood off and fired broadsides of cannon to inflict maximum damage to fabric and men. The brave Juan

Martinez de Recalde in the largest Spanish galleon the *San Juan de Portugal* turned to meet the attack and sought to grapple with one of the three English ships. The English ships skilfully kept their distance and pounded the *San Juan* from about 300 yards for about an hour. The constant boom of cannon was clearly heard from the shore at Plymouth. Fortunately for the Spanish ships much of the cannon fire fell short, and that which did hit the target inflicted little damage. This was because cannon balls did not explode like modern shells. They could only inflict impact damage and so the sinking of a ship was very rare. The *Gran Grin* raced to the rescue of the *San Juan* and the Armada slowed to enable the *San Juan* to catch up and take refuge inside the Spanish crescent. The English ships veered away and made sure that they kept the advantage of the wind direction. Martin was in the forefront of the four-hour engagement and while the *Triumph* was cumbersome, his seamanship and fighting qualities were exemplary. An extract from one account of the battle states, "This day saw the fiercest action against the Armada. The greatest battle the English had fought at sea. It lasted from morning until night. Frobisher was first to enter it and the last to leave. He was the hero of that memorable day".[22] However, after a long-range furious bombardment, little harm was done to either side. The *San Juan* sustained most damage but had been able to return to the shelter of her fleet for repairs. So the Armada sailed passed Plymouth almost unharmed and moved on eastwards along the Channel towards its rendezvous with the Duke of Parma.

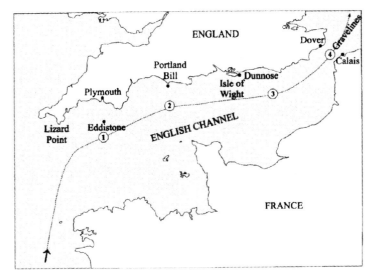

Progress of the Armada along the English Channel. The numbers indicate where Martin's major actions took place.

1. First day's attack and bombardment off the Eddistone Rock, Plymouth

2. The *Triumph's* isolation and battle with the Spanish Flagship off Portland Bill.

3. Martin outwits Medina Sidonia in the Spanish Flagship off Dunnose Head, Isle of Wight.

4. The fireships and the decisive battle of Gravelines off Calais.

That night two incidents occurred which caused more damage to the Spanish ships than all the English cannon balls had done. The first was when one ship was the victim of a terrible accident when the gunpowder stored astern accidentally exploded. The second was when the *Rosario* collided with another ship and was so seriously damaged that she lost speed and couldn't keep up with the Armada. An attempt to tow her failed and reluctantly she had to be left behind to drift helplessly as the weather worsened. Observing the *Rosario's* predicament Howard gave strict orders to all the ship's captains that she was not to be pursued. He stressed that it was far more important for the English fleet to keep together so that they were ready to engage the enemy the next day.

Howard now waited for the ships that had not as yet managed to leave Plymouth. He appointed Drake to head the line of English ships tracking the Armada and instructed him to keep his lantern lit all night so that it acted as a marker for the other ships to follow. This would ensure that they stayed together and would be in range to attack the Armada the next day. Sir Francis was a gallant and famous hero, whose exploits had won him a nation-wide reputation but the lure of treasure overcame his call to duty. He disobeyed Howard's orders, doused his lantern, abandoned his post and went after the *Rosario.* When challenged, captain Valdes surrendered without a fight and Drake claimed the *Rosario* as his prize. This was considerable because she had the royal money chest stowed on board. She was taken into Dartmouth so that Drake could later share out his ill-gotten gains. The result of his disobedience was that by dawn the English ships were scattered and some were in great danger. Howard in the *Ark Royal* found himself in a very vulnerable position. He was almost inside the Spanish crescent and only just managed to extricate himself and two other ships that were with him. Because Drake had doused his lantern Howard had mistakenly followed the lantern of the Spanish flagship thinking it was Drake's lantern. Drake's misdemeanour meant that the whole of the next day was lost while the English fleet reassembled. Drake made a lame excuse about seeing some ships which he went to investigate but there is no doubt that his fellow commanders were not amused. Martin was perhaps the one who was most annoyed at Drake's action, which had put so much at risk. He is reported to have said later at Harwich "...He (Drake) had seen her (*the Rosario*) in the evening, that she had spent her masts, then like a coward, he kept by her all night, because he would have the spoil. He thinketh to cozen (cheat) us of our shares of fifteen thousand ducketts, but we will have our shares, or I will make him spend the best blood in his belly....".[23] The forthright Yorkshireman had a valid point but he was not very diplomatic to say it in those terms, and certainly not in the presence of Lord Howard and John Hawkins. Drake's reputation however was never quite the same after this shameful episode

Martin was heavily involved in the next major action on Tuesday 2nd August off Portland Bill. The English commanders were convinced that Medina Sidonia intended to find a landing place on the South Coast, probably in the Solent in the shelter of the Isle of White. This would enable him to replenish his supplies and liaise with the Duke of Parma across the Channel. Philip had forbidden such a landing but Medina Sidonia was by now anxious to do so. The English had reviewed the first day's action and had noted that firing at long distance was for the most part ineffective. They had to get much closer to the enemy if they were to inflict any serious damage on them. The wind changed to the north-east which for the first time gave the advantage of the wind gauge to the Spanish. Beyond Portland Bill lay the harbours of Portland and Weymouth. These were excellent landing grounds. Lord Howard sought to block the way but the wind was against him, and the Spanish were set to arrive at Portland first. Martin in the *Triumph* along with five armed merchantmen had become detached from the fleet and was stationed in the lee of the Bill. Sidonia in the *San Martin* and four huge galleases broke away from their formation and moved in to attack the *Triumph*. She must have seemed like a "sitting duck" to them. This was especially so because the galleases were the Spaniards' most heavily armed vessels and had oars as well as sails. They were therefore more manoeuvrable and not so dependent on the wind. Each had at least fifty guns and around 200 soldiers and they were specially designed to grapple with and to board an enemy ship so that their soldiers could overpower the defenders by fighting it out on her decks.

Photograph of the tidal race off Portland Bill.

Things looked extremely bleak for the *Triumph* at that moment. Martin was seriously outnumbered and outgunned. He could have tried to escape but this was not part of his character. He decided to engage the enemy and would out-manoeuvre them by taking full advantage of his knowledge of the very strong tidal currents around Portland Bill. He also knew that his gunners could fire far more frequently than the enemy. The Spanish attacked, firing broadside after broadside at the *Triumph*. Martin responded by turning broadside and getting in really close. At very close range his gunners fired fusillade after fusillade of iron shot and stones, especially from his lower guns, into the *San Martin*. The *Triumph* had forty-one guns and twenty-six quick firers. It was all or nothing, and the Spaniards were outwitted and outfought. When the galleases tried to grapple and board, Martin with uncanny seamanship, kept yardarm to yardarm, and held them off. All the while his gunners pounded them with the *Triumph's* ordnance. The effect of firing low and at very close range caused mayhem aboard the galleases. Many oarsmen were wounded or killed and their oars rendered useless. Some think that this was an entirely new tactic of naval warfare. It was certainly effective and the Spanish found that it was they who were fighting for survival. Martin's brilliant seamanship and fighting strategies were unrivalled on that day. The battle went on for nearly two hours until a change in wind direction enabled Lord Howard in the *Ark Royal* to lead a line of seven ships to "rescue" the *Triumph*. He bore down on the *San Martin*. Her proud Holy Banner was shot through, her masts and rigging were seriously damaged and she was holed above and below the waterline. Martin had given her a real pounding. Sidonia had been thoroughly beaten and he withdrew along with the galleases. He joined the rest of his fleet to lick his wounds and to fight another day. All the while the other English squadrons had been harrying and attacking the rear of the Spanish crescent and by the end of the day it had proved to be a very decisive engagement in favour of the English.

Historians have postulated many theories as to how and why Martin had become detached from the main fleet. Was it a deliberate ploy to coax the Spanish into the dangerous tides and shoals of the area? Was he acting under orders to protect

the coast, especially Portland, Weymouth and Torbay, and thus
to prevent any of the Spaniards from landing? Could it be that
when the wind changed the *Triumph* was so cumbersome and
so positioned that she could not tack quickly enough to follow Howard when the rest of the fleet changed tack? Was he
trying to draw away some of the galleases and galleons so that
the Armada's formation was broken and vulnerable to attack by
others? Who knows? The main thing is that the Armada was
delayed, diverted and pushed further and further from the coast
by a line of about fifty English ships. Howard regrouped and
with a favourable wind continued to harry and pound the flagship of Medina Sidonia. Whatever the truth, Martin's contribution to that day had given the advantage to the English.

The next day, Wednesday 3rd August, was spent in repairing
damage and replenishing supplies. All the while volunteers from
the Channel ports in all sorts of boats were constantly joining
the fleet. The commanders met and the English fleet was divided
into four squadrons under the commands of Howard, Frobisher,
Drake and Hawkins. This new order would give greater control
and would allow their attacks to be far more effective. Martin
was in command of the landward squadron and was to deny
the Spaniards a safe harbour at the Isle of Wight and beyond.
He quickly grasped the initiative and on Thursday 4th August
he was off Dunnose Head on the Isle of Wight from where he
was able to blockade the entrance to the Solent. He was now
ahead of the Spanish and must have towed his squadron and
the *Triumph* during the night, using pinnaces and small boats.
In the morning he found himself near to the flagship *San Martin* again. He immediately opened fire. Unfortunately the wind
freshened from the south-west and enabled a number of Spanish galleons to come to the rescue of their flagship. The *Triumph*
found herself in dire peril once again because she was so close

inshore that there was little room to manoeuvre and the *Triumph* was no match for the approaching galleons. Fortunately the rest of his squadron were some way off and managed to escape from the impending threat. The wind was light so Martin quickly had his small boats launched to tow the *Triumph* out of danger. Other ships sent their boats to help and soon eleven rowboats were towing the *Triumph*. Suddenly the wind strengthened and Martin in record speed set his sails to catch it and sailed out of danger. Sailors from both sides marvelled at the speed and the expert way in which this was done. Medina Sidonia and his captains were sure this was their best opportunity to grapple and board the *Triumph* and with full sail they attacked. Sidonia wrote later "We made certain that we would this day succeed in boarding them, which was the only way to victory"[24]. They never got near because Martin with tremendous skill left all the galleons in the *Triumph's* wake. A ship's officer wrote, "She got out so swiftly that the galleon *San Juan* and another quick-sailing ship (the speediest vessels in the Armada) seemed in comparison with her to be standing still".[25]

Medina Sidonia had been diverted again having left his fleet and by Martin's brave and astute actions the Armada had temporarily been without its Commander in Chief. When Sidonia returned to his fleet it was to see it being constantly harried by the squadrons of Drake and Hawkins. The crescent was all the while being pushed further and further inshore and northwards towards Selsey Bill, beyond the Solent, where the treacherous Ower Banks lie just beneath the surface. To avoid running aground and certain shipwreck, Medina Sidonia had to redirect the Armada away from the coast. This forced change of direction proved decisive because the Armada was never again in a position to land on English soil. The next morning, recognising the previous day's battle as a victory, Lord Howard called

Bernard Finegan Gribble, *Knighting the Captains on Board the Ark Royal*, 1936. Courtesy of The National Trust, Buckland Abbey. Copyright photograph Sotheby's of London.

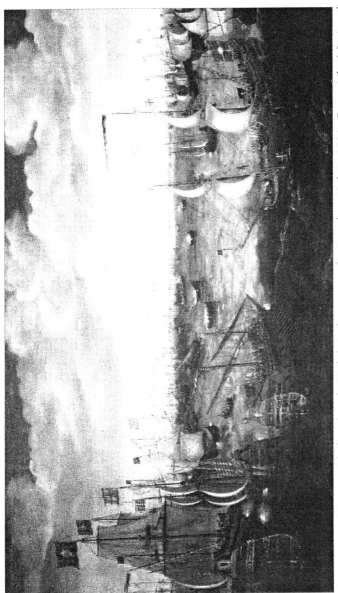

Antonisz & Vroom, *The launch of the English fireships against the Armada at Calais, 1588*. Copyright National Maritime Museum, London.

Martin Frobisher, Thomas Howard and John Hawkins to the *Ark Royal*, where with deep gratitude he knighted them all. He was pleased to do so, because knighthoods were often conferred at Court to rather dubious recipients, merely because of their social standing. In this case, their peers, in the fray of battle had witnessed the bravery and true valour of these new knights.

There followed a lull in the fighting and the Spanish fleet crossed the Channel and anchored at Calais. The English ships anchored nearby and Howard called Lord Henry Seymour to join him with his thirty or so ships from Dover. This brought the English Fleet up to about 140. One of Seymour's captains, Sir William Winter suggested sending fireships into the Spanish fleet while it was at anchor and very vulnerable. Howard agreed to this tactic. On Sunday 7th August some merchant ships were prepared for the purpose by filling them with flammable materials. Their guns were loaded and primed for firing so that they would be discharged when the flames reached them. The noise of the cannon firing would add to the psychological impact of the tactic. They were let loose at night with the wind and tide behind them. When the Spaniards saw the fireships in the darkness and coming towards them they were terrified because all sailors dreaded fire on board their ships probably more than anything else. They were even more terrified in case the fireships were floating bombs similar to the fearsome hellburners of Antwerp which were still very fresh in people's memories. These were ships full of explosives that were set on fire and sent unmanned amongst the enemy to explode with catastrophic results. Sidonia immediately took preventative action and sent out some small boats which bravely intercepted the fireships and succeeded in towing two of them off their course and out of harm's way. He ordered all the captains to weigh anchor quickly and, except for one collision, the Armada moved northwards towards Dunkirk. In its hasty departure from Calais the Armada could not re-form into its defensive crescent and as it left Calais it was more vulnerable than at any time previously. Sidonia must have realised by that stage that the possibility of a rendezvous with Parma was fast receding.

As dawn broke on Monday 8th August the Armada, having lost the initiative and its defensive shape presented the English with their best opportunity to attack and inflict substantial damage on it. Instead of pressing home this advantage Lord Howard (like Drake before him) forsook his post to claim a grounded galleas as his prize. Not so Frobisher, Drake and Hawkins; they went straight on the attack with Lord Seymour's squadron in support. The battle off Gravelines had begun. Drake in the *Revenge* led the first charge and chose the flagship *San Martin* as his target. He sailed close and came to within half a musket shot range, (about one hundred yards), turned and fired his bow guns and then turned again to fire his broadside guns. The *San Martin* returned fire and the *Revenge* was so close that she was hit and "pierced through by cannon balls of all sizes". The rest of Drake's squadron followed and loosed off their broadsides. Inexplicably Drake then left the attack and sailed away to the Northeast with his squadron. Was this because the *Revenge* had been hit by so much shot that she had incurred a lot of damage and needed time to recover? Had Drake seen some other opportunity that caused him to change his tactics? Martin didn't know the cause of Drake's actions but he was furious with him. He later vented his anger at Harwich, "He (Drake) came bragging up at the first indeed and gave them his prow and his broadside; and then kept his luff (part of the foresail), and was glad that he was gone again like a cowardly knave or traitor—I rest doubtful, but the one I will swear".[26] Some think Martin should have left the *San Martin* and followed Drake. It is conjecture of course, but if Drake had remained and fought on with the other squadrons, they would probably have captured or at least disabled the flagship of Medina Sidonia. This would have been a tremendous military and psychological blow to the enemy. With his usual single-mindedness Martin stayed and pressed home the attack on the *San Martin*. He pursued her and ferociously bombarded her, with his cannon pouring broadside after broadside into her from as close a range as possible but always avoiding grappling. Hawkins, aware of the importance of the skirmish, arrived in the *Victory* to join in the attack. Seeing the plight of Sidonia's flagship, other Spanish ships came to her aid and joined in the fighting. The range got closer and closer until the ships were so close together that men were firing muskets at each other from the decks. The *San Martin* was hit at least 200 times and sustained major damage to its hull and rigging. Other Spanish ships closed in and came to the rescue and gradually the Armada was able to form its crescent shape again, thus protecting the flagship. As the English continued their attacks the Spanish ships had to take drastic defensive actions and alter their courses. The result was that in escaping from the English some of them collided with each other often causing more damage than had been caused by the English cannon balls. The outcome of this brutal engagement was that hundreds of Spaniards had been killed or wounded and many of the Spanish ships were badly damaged and some say that at least three were sunk. It would have been much worse for them if the English had not run very low on supplies and ammunition. As it was, the Armada never recovered from the onslaught of that day. Dejected and demoralised, the Spanish fleet sailed northwards and unfortunately for them was heading straight for new and hidden dangers from submerged sandbanks.

The next day could have seen the demise of the Armada as

it desperately tried to avoid the sandbanks. They were almost upon them and at the mercy of the English and fully expected to perish. Luis de Miranda wrote, "We saw ourselves lost or taken by the enemy, or the whole Armada drowned upon the banks. It was the most fearful day in the world, for the whole company had lost all hope of success and looked only for death. But it pleased God to blind the enemy so that he did not fall on us, and to work a miracle in preserving us from such a disaster".[27] Sidonia took confession and wrote later "God alone can rescue them." He must have thought his prayer was answered for almost immediately the wind freshened from the Southwest and the fleet was able to veer away from the dreaded sandbanks and head into the North Sea. Meanwhile Howard sent Seymour (much to his displeasure) back to Dover to guard the Narrow Seas and the rest were content to merely follow the Armada at a distance. On Friday 12th August Medina Sidonia gave orders for the fleet to sail round the North of Scotland and then to alter course and sail southwards down the west coast of Ireland and then home to Spain. Having passed round Scotland they turned south to sail down the West Coast of Ireland. Here they encountered foul weather conditions and many ships were wrecked in the violent storms. In the famous words of Elizabeth "God blew with His wind and they were scattered." It is estimated that at least 11,000 Spaniards lost their lives in the doomed invasion of England. The battle of the Spanish Armada was over and England was safe, but she was not complacent and remained on guard. At Tilbury the Queen met with her Army which the Earl of Leicester had mustered. News about the defeat of the Armada at sea had not yet reached them and they were still expecting the invasion to succeed and that Parma's army would soon arrive on English soil to march on London. Her historic speech that day stirred the heart of every Englishman:

"Let tyrants fear. I have always so behaved myself that, under God, I have placed my chiefest strength and safeguard in the loyal hearts and good will of my subjects; and therefore I am come amongst you as you see, at this time, not for my recreation and disport, but being resolved, in the midst and heat of battle, to live or die amongst you all, and to lay down for my God, and for my kingdom, and for my people, my honour and my blood, even in the dust. I know I have the body of a weak and feeble woman, but I have the heart and stomach of a king, and of a king of England too, and think foul scorn of that Parma or Spain, or any prince of Europe should dare to invade the borders of my realm..." [28]

The Spaniards had dared but the few who returned to Spain must have wished otherwise. The English navy, her Commanders, Sir Martin Frobisher among them, and their gallant and brave seamen had under God and their Queen, prevailed. England had been spared a bloody invasion and Elizabeth was still Queen of her realm with all that it meant for her people and the Protestant Church.

The aftermath of the Armada campaign however led to many unfortunate and sad consequences. The ship's companies were not stood down in case of further danger but they were unpaid and impoverished and many died of disease or malnutrition. The Commanders continued their recriminations about their actions and their unequal remuneration. Drake was not popular with many of his peers and especially with Martin. Even Philip of Spain had a report that the differences between Drake and Frobisher still continued. One can understand these tensions when Drake received £4000 as his share of the *Rosario* prize on top of his other payments. Martin was paid 20 shillings a day for when he was at sea and about £5000 for his part in the defeat of the Armada. Out of this he had to pay many expenses which after paying left him with very little. What he had gained was an enhanced reputation while Drake's had inevitably declined because of his greed and dereliction of duty. No one had been more involved or had fought with more valour and skill than Martin.

It was at this time in 1588 that he heard sadly from London that his wife Isabel (nee Riggatt) whom he had married in 1559 had died. She had been living in very poor and wretched circumstances in London and it does not seem that Martin had provided sufficiently for her needs nor cared for her as he ought. It must have been a very hard life for the wives of seafarers in those days when their husbands were away for so often and for so long. "Out of sight, out of mind" did not excuse him but probably partly explains his neglect. Certainly Martin, probably short of money, did not make adequate provision for her. She was buried at her hometown of Snaith in East Yorkshire.

Spain had been humbled at sea but the Queen and Lord Howard had to consider how best to protect England from any further threat. Lord Howard therefore went to London and left Sir Martin, Sir William Winter and Sir John Hawkins in command of the fleet. He appointed Sir Henry Palmer to command the eight ships patrolling the channel and Martin was ordered to take over from him after two months had elapsed. In the meantime he remained in command of the *Triumph* until 15th September when he transferred to the *Revenge.* He patrolled the channel disrupting Spanish supplies as they headed towards Philip's armies in the Low Countries. On 1st January 1589 he transferred to the *Vanguard* and took command of the eight ships guarding the channel. During this time he once again began to capture foreign ships and claimed them as prizes.

There was confusion as to what was a legitimate target for privateers and what was piracy. Martin, rightly or wrongly, exploited this to his own advantage. Many legal claims were made against him but he always managed to escape any consequences. Indeed the Privy Council itself often turned a blind eye to his actions. The result was that Martin prospered and his wealth grew. He bought property at Tower Hill in London where his wares were traded and brought in a large income.

He was not only in the business of seizing ships for plunder. He was always on the look out for spies whose information would be of benefit to the Crown. Thus his knowledge of the enemy and his reputation grew. He was after all one of the four chief commanders who defeated the Armada. In the meantime, Sir Francis' reputation continued to decline. He and Norrey had returned after a disastrous voyage to Corunna, which cost the Queen dear and so incurred her displeasure. Spain was still a threat and was replenishing her treasury from across the Atlantic. The only way to actively inhibit this was to capture the treasure ships on the high seas. On 30th August 1589 Martin was commissioned to command the *Elizabeth Bonaventure* and to lead a flotilla of ships to search for and capture Spanish treasure ships. He headed south and stood off Cape Sagras, at the very tip of Southwest Spain, watching for any approaching treasure ships. It was not long before he spotted them. Unfortunately they were ships designed for speed and Martin's ships could not keep pace with them and so most of them escaped. He had to be content with seizing four of them and headed back for England. Further misfortune meant that, in a storm off Eddistone, two of them sank with their precious cargoes. Martin, with his customary concern for human life, stopped and pulled the drowning sailors from the sea. The plunder from the two surviving ships made the trip worthwhile but it could have been so much better.

Martin returned to his duties commanding the fleet guarding the Channel. He brought back Lord Willoughby's ailing army from Cherbourg and then in March 1590 he was appointed as joint Commander of a fleet with Hawkins. Their orders were to intercept Spanish treasure ships returning to Spain but it was not until June that they were able to set sail. Martin went out into the Atlantic near the Azores while Hawkins stationed himself off the Portuguese coast. Martin patrolled for a month without success and returned to Plymouth empty-handed. It was another example of a voyage having to finish prematurely because of stingy victualling. Hawkins returned with a little more success but the enterprise must have made a loss. It did have one important outcome. Spain was beginning to suffer financially because of the constant attention the English were giving to seizing her ships. Martin was convinced of this strategy and strongly commended it to the higher powers. If England could not have the gold, then deny it to Spain, was his argument.

In March 1591 Lord Howard, in the *Defiance*, with Sir Richard Grenville as vice admiral in the *Revenge*, led a squadron to cruise off the Azores to intercept Spanish treasure galleons. The Spanish were now slowly recovering from the debacle of 1588 and sent out a strong flotilla of warships to protect their galleons. Howard and Grenville did not expect to be attacked by the Spanish from the East and in the ensuing battle the *Revenge* was overcome, boarded and captured. Grenville and his men had fought furiously, even sinking two enemy ships, but it was to no avail. Grenville died three days later and the *Revenge* sank in a storm. The remaining men were taken prisoner and to their credit the Spaniards treated them well. When the news of the demise of the *Revenge* and the heroism of Grenville and his crew reached England, it had a profound effect. It stirred the hearts of Englishmen to even greater efforts to diminish the power of Spain. The result was a profusion of licences granted to English privateers. Not only did they want to degrade Spanish power by harassing and capturing their ships; they wanted to seek their own fortunes as well.

Martin, now quite wealthy, went to Altofts where he bought various properties and lived as a country gentleman running his estates. He married a widow, Dame Dorothy Wentworth, daughter of Lord Wentworth. She was a mature lady with one grown up daughter. This liaison gave him a ready made family but denied him the possibility of fathering any children. It was at this time that he became a justice of the peace and built Frobisher Hall.

In the spring of 1592 the Queen sponsored another voyage which had two aims. Firstly it was to sail down the coast of Spain to seek out and destroy any Spanish ships that might be used for another Armada, and secondly they were to take as prizes any Spanish treasure ships returning from the Spanish Main. Sir Walter Raleigh was appointed to command the fleet with Sir John Burgh as his vice admiral. The fleet set sail from Plymouth in early May 1592 but the Queen changed her mind and relieved Sir Walter of his command. Sir Martin was ordered to replace him and he took command of the voyage (This shows how much confidence the Queen now had in him). Sir Walter was ordered to return to England immediately but he disobeyed and went with the fleet as far as Spain, returning to England a fortnight later, (He was later jailed by the Queen for daring to marry one of her ladies-in-waiting). Martin divided the fleet into two squadrons. Burgh took one and patrolled near the Azores and Martin cruised along the Spanish Coast. Martin's squadron found very few ships to seize but Burgh, now reinforced with other privateers, spotted a huge Spanish ship on the horizon.

She was the *Madre de Dios,* a 1600-ton well armed merchant ship. She put up a furious fight but the English boarded her and she was soon in their hands. She was laden with a fabulous cargo of gold, precious jewels, spices and clothes, which were estimated to be worth at least £500,000, a huge sum in those days and already the object of greedy eyes.

Burgh set off for England with his very valuable prize. The accompanying ship's crews could not overcome the temptation and they took every opportunity to pilfer from the captured treasure. With their valuables burning holes in their pockets they raced ahead to get back to England before Burgh. Many of the ships went to Portsmouth and the hostelries saw intense business as sailors sold their portions of precious loot. Burgh headed for Dartmouth harbour and word soon got around that a captured Spanish treasure ship was on its way. Martin was unaware of these developments but had been informed that the Spanish did not intend to risk sending any more treasure ships that year. When he did get news about the *Madre de Dios* he made all speed to intercept Burgh before he could reach port. He was unsuccessful and it must have been extremely galling for him, the Commander of the voyage, to arrive later at Dartmouth to find much of the treasure had already disappeared via a myriad of hands. It would certainly not have been allowed to happen if he had brought the *Madre de Dios* back. Only about £140,000 worth of booty remained from an original total valued at £500,000. Sir Walter Raleigh was sent from jail to stop the pilfering. Sir Francis Drake had already tried to stop it but he could do nothing because the men thought that they were only doing what Drake had spent most of his life doing. Robert Cecil was sent as a Commissioner and everyone he met in the Exeter area, who carried a bag or had a coat, smelled of amber, musk and other materials taken from the prize anchored in Dartmouth harbour.

Martin no doubt received some share of the spoils, as well as his 30s a day for wages, but it was a financially disappointing end to the saga for him. There is no account of Martin's response to the authorities at Dartmouth or to Captain Burgh and his crews. It may be that his intemperate nature had matured with age but one cannot help surmising that many would incur his wrath and be subjected to a verbal lashing, if not worse.

CHAPTER 9

MARTIN'S LAST BATTLE

The Spanish Armada had been routed, their ships had been seized and plundered but the war was not won. England just did not have the capability or the resources to defeat the might of the Spanish Empire totally. The only thing Queen Elizabeth could do was to be vigilant and to degrade Spanish power at sea whenever her navy could. Philip realised that he needed to control a port in France, nearer to the English coast if he was ever to launch another invasion. He chose Brest on the Northwest tip of France. On learning of this the Queen and her advisors decided that this new threat had to be attacked and extinguished. Who was to command this sea and land attack? She chose Sir Martin, who was in her favour, not so much for his social standing as for his record in obeying and achieving her instructions. She trusted him to get the job done and wrote to him on 25th February 1594, "To Sir Martin Frobisher, These shall be to require you immediately upon sight hereof to make your repair hither, where at your coming you shall further understand the cause where you are sent for and so not doubting of your performance hereof. We bid you etc. etc.". [29]

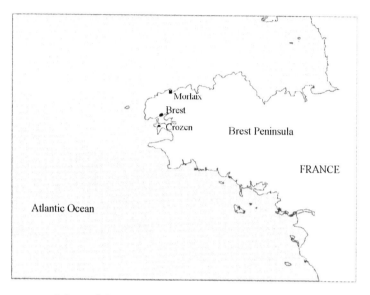

Map of the Brest Peninsula, Northern France

He was made Admiral of a fleet of five royal ships, the *Vanguard, Rainbow, Crane, Quittance* and *Moon.* An army of some of Elizabeth's best soldiers, under the command of Norrey, was to accompany the ships. On 27th August 1594 the fleet set sail from the Thames to support the French land army which had already attacked Brest but had only been partially successful. The problem was that the Spanish had built a fort near Crozen on the Crozen Peninsula overlooking the approach to Brest harbour. It had excellent defences and held out against all attacks. Norrey's soldiers were landed at Paimpol, about seventy miles to the East, because there were no easy landing places near to Brest. Rather than wasting time waiting for Norrey to march to Brest, Martin sailed to Morlaix on the northern coast of the Brest Peninsula and attacked the town. He landed a siege train and then ordered his ships to sail past the town with all their guns showing. This had the desired affect and the town immediately surrendered and the French soldiers took possession of it. This was a brilliant engagement, for it meant that Norrey was not delayed on his long march and it was accomplished without losing a single man or wasting ordnance.

On 6th September all was ready for the assault on the fort. It was always going to be a very difficult and dangerous engagement because the Spanish garrison under the command of Colonel Juan del Anguila had all the advantages. After Martin's ships had taken on fresh supplies he began a bombardment of the fort with cannon but the walls were so well constructed that his shot did little damage. Meanwhile other problems were escalating. Sir John Norrey's army marching over land had made slow progress and only arrived on October 1st. The weather had turned against them making the roads into rivers of mud and their slow progress meant that they were short of supplies. Consequently, many of the soldiers had fallen ill and were not in a fit state to fight. Also the siege train had not yet arrived by sea from Morlaix. An initial exploratory attack on 9th October failed to make any impact. It was only on 23rd October that the siege train arrived and it was set up to bombard the fort. Norrey decided to attack the outskirts of the fort to prevent their gunners from firing at his troops. This attack was disastrous and many men were wounded and some killed. Further unsuccessful action, bad weather and disease eroded morale and the French commander suggested lifting the siege. Martin was outraged. He wrote to Howard and Burghley "I am ashamed to write to your honours of these delays of the French. For this present day we should have battered and assaulted it by an agreement made betwixt ourselves".[30] Eventually the French agreed to maintain the siege and to carry out further attacks.

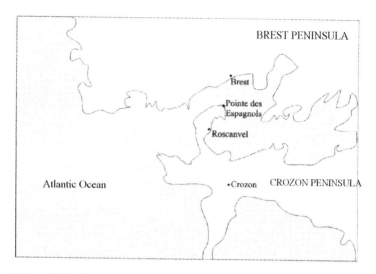

BREST PENINSULA

•Brest

•Pointe des
Espagnols

•Roscanvel

Atlantic Ocean

•Crozon   CROZON PENINSULA

Map of the Crozen Peninsula opposite Brest, Northern France

The wall of the fort was 37 feet thick. Little wonder it sustained little damage from cannon balls. Other means had to be used. During the night explosives were laid under part of the fort's wall. Immediately after the explosion Martin and the French commander personally led their men in the charge towards the breach in the wall. They were running straight towards the fort's main defensive guns. The English gunners concentrated their fire on the breach and many Spaniards died in the hail of bullets. In the following melee someone opened the main gate. Martin and his men were closest to the gate and he immediately took advantage of this good fortune and led his men through it. A bloody battle followed as Martin and his men forced the enemy back. For five hours they were involved in fierce hand to hand fighting and many defenders were slaughtered. Towards the end of the battle some of the Spaniards turned and jumping from the fort's walls into the sea they swam to the

English ships hoping to be taken safely on board. Their hopes were in vain because the mariners on the ships simply held the poor Spaniards under the water until they drowned. Of the 400 brave soldiers defending the fort only 9 were taken prisoner. They were released and went back to their commander who immediately had them hanged for cowardice. About sixty Englishmen died that day and many were wounded, including Martin and Norrey.

Martin wrote to Howard, "By a battery, undermining, and a very dangerous assault we have taken this fort, with the loss of our people but none of any account. They defended it very resolutely and never asked for mercy, so were put all to the sword saving five or six who hid themselves. ... We are about to get in our ordnance as fast as we can and so to make our repair homeward. ... I was shot in with a bullet along the huckle bone so I was driven to have an incision made to take out the bullet. So as I am neither to go nor ride, and the mariners are very willing to go except I go with them myself, yet if we had victuals it were easily done, but here is none to be had..." [31] (spellings in modern form). Martin again laments the fact that supplies determined the length and effectiveness of his voyages. Therefore he set sail for home as the Queen had ordered. The expedition was a total success. The port of Brest was no longer a threat to Elizabeth's Realm.

While it is true that the fort is often identified as the fort at Crozen it was actually built on the Crozen Peninsula at Roscanvel, near to Crozon, in a place that is still called "Place of the Spaniards". The Spaniards had named the fort "Castil Leon," the "Castle of the Lion". The fort was eventually completely destroyed and there are no traces of it today as other fortifications have been built where it once stood.

The ships left Brest and set sail for Plymouth on 12th November. When they arrived, Martin's wound had become infected and he was in great pain. The surgeon who had removed the bullet had probably left some wadding in the wound that had festered or perhaps the equipment that he had used wasn't sterile. The wound being near the hip could not be treated by amputation and the infection spread. Martin probably knew his end had come long before arriving at Plymouth. Unlike many of his compatriots who died at sea or in foreign lands he died in his beloved England on 15th November 1594. He died, making the ultimate sacrifice in the service of his country, amongst those he had led and commanded with such distinction; ordinary seafaring men with whom he had served and who in return had served him and his Queen so well. Following his death after his last battle for Elizabeth and England one chronicler wrote; "Neither was this victory gotten by the English without bloode. Sir Martin Frobisher wounded with a small shot in the hip brought his fleet back to Plymouth and then died. A valorious and stout man he was, and to be among the most famousest men of our age, for counsel and conduct, and glory gotten by naval exploits, as by what I have before spoken of him plainly appeareth".[32]

CHAPTER 10

MARTIN REMEMBERED

The very day before he died, Queen Elizabeth wrote to him in her own handwriting. The letter of appreciation shows how much his reputation had grown and how she now esteemed him:

"Trustie and well beloved, we greet you well. We have seen your letter to our treasurer and our Admyrall and thereby perceive your love of our service, also by others your owne good carriage, whereby you have won yourself reputation: whereof for that wee imagine it will be comforting unto you to understand wee have thought good to vouchsafe to take knowledge of it by our own handwriting. We know you are sufficiently instructed from our Admyrall, besides your own circumspection howe to prevent any soddaine mischief by fire or otherwise upon our Fleet under your charge and yet do wee think it will worke in you the more impression, to be by ourself remembered again, who have observed by former experience that the Spaniards, for all their boaste, will trust more to their devices than they dare in deed with force look upon you.

For the rest of my directions wee leave them to such letters as you shall receive from our Counsaile. Given under our Privie Signet at our mansion of Richmond

the 14th November in the Thirty Sixth yeare of our
Reigne 1594
To our Trustie and well beloved
Sir Martin Furbissher, Knight". [33]

Sadly, Martin died before he could read this personal letter
of commendation from his Queen.

After his death his body was prepared for burial. His inter-
nal soft organs were removed and buried in St Andrew's Church,
Plymouth. The rest of his corpse was embalmed and it was decided that it should be taken to London for burial. This seems
rather strange as his usual home and estates were in the area
of Altofts in Yorkshire. However, it would not have been easy
to transport the body to Altofts because it meant a very long
overland journey or a sea journey to a Yorkshire port followed
by a land journey inland to Altofts. Martin had lived for some
of the time in London at a house in Beech Street located in the
parish of St Giles' Church, Cripplegate. This qualified him to
be buried there and it was probably easier to take his corpse to
London rather than Altofts especially if it was taken via the sea
and the Thames. Whether by land or sea his corpse was laid to
rest in the south aisle of this London church.

St Giles' Church, Cripplegate, London.

It is a strange quirk of history that both churches housing his remains should receive direct hits from German bombs in the blitzes of the Second World War. Both Churches were devastated and then restored after the war was over. A memorial tablet in the side chapel at St Andrew's refers to the Parish Register for 22nd November 1594. The entry in the registry reads: "Sir Martayne Frobisher knight being wounded at the Fort built againste Brest by the Spanyerdes deceased at Plymouth the 15th November whose entralls were heere enterred but his corpes were carried home to be buried in London."

Many historians and the memorial tablet at St Andrew's state that he died on the 22nd November 1594 but in actual fact he died on 15th November and his soft organs were buried in St Andrew's on the 22nd November. Martin shares the tablet with another famous English Mariner, Admiral Robert Blake who died in 1657 within sight of Plymouth and whose body was given the same treatment as Martin's and his corpse then transferred to London to be buried in Westminster Abbey.

St Andrew's Church, Plymouth.

Interior of St Andrew's Church, Plymouth.

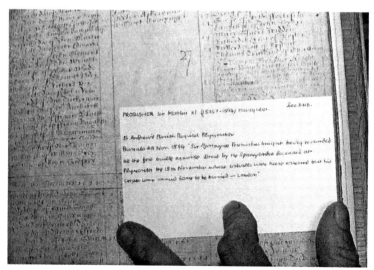

Extract from St Andrew's Parish Register 1594.

Memorial Tablet in St Andrew's Church, Plymouth.

All Saints Church, Normanton. Martin Frobisher's Parish Church.

On a visit to Normanton while researching his family history, George Frobisher (the author's father and direct descendent of Sir Martin's brother Davey) was surprised that Sir Martin's Parish Church had no monument to his memory. He decided that this was a serious omission, especially as Martin's funeral service was held there. He formed a Trust and in conjunction with the authorities of All Saints Church, family members and others, set about raising funds for a stained glass window to be put in the church in Sir Martin's memory. Harry Harvey of York was commissioned to design it and it was dedicated on July 15th 1978. The window consists of Sir Martin's Coat of Arms, a chalice, an Elizabethan ship, an iceberg, two anchors and his family motto FORTE AJUVAT IPSE DEUS (God himself helps the brave). All are symbolic of Martin's exploits.

Memorial window in All Saints Parish Church, Normanton.
The inscription beside the window reads:

Sir Martin Frobisher, Kt.,
Of Altofts, 1535-1594
Admiral of the Fleet, Explorer, Navigator. Seeker of
the North West Passage to Cathay (China) 1576.7.8.

Discoverer of Frobisher Straits, Baffin Island. Knighted at sea for services against the Spanish Armada. He
died of wounds suffered in the attack and capture of
the Fort at Crozen, Brest Peninsula.
He was buried in the church of St Giles, Cripplegate,
London, but his funeral service was conducted at his
own request, "At my own Parish Church of Normanton." He introduced the Anglican Communion Service to the North American Continent on his last voyage of Discovery in the Year 1578.

Martin made his Last Will and Testament whilst at sea in
1594. He dictated his wishes to his Gentleman at Arms who
warned him against making his nephew Peter his main heir because he considered him to be a weak willed man and lacking in
integrity. Martin would not change his mind and is reputed to
have said that as the Will was made at sea it would not last long
on land. How right he was because Peter did not manage the
inheritance wisely and it was soon dissipated. He even incurred
a fine of 20 shillings for entering into his inheritance without
the consent of Queen Elizabeth, which was not a good omen.
The Will, which was read out in the porch of All Saints Church,
Normanton sometime after the funeral is a very long document
to include here but begins (changed into modern English):

"In the name of God. Amen The...day of...in the year
of our Lord God one thousand, five hundred, ninety
and four I Martin Frobisher Knight being in perfect
health and of good remembrance thanked be almighty
god, with good advice and consideration do make
and ordain this my last will and testament in writing
in manner and form following. That is to say First I

commend my soul into the hands of almighty god my maker, hoping assuredly through the only merits of Jesus Christ my saviour and redeemer to be made partaker of life everlasting And as concerning my body I commend it to my mother the earth from whence it came to be interred where it shall please god to call me at the discretion and disposition of my Executor. But my will and mind is, that the solemnisation of my funeral shall be kept at the parish Church of Normanton and my house called Frobisher Hall in Altofts in the county of York. As touching provision to be had and made for Dame Dorothy my wellbeloved wife by this my last will and testament, my will and mind is, and by these presents I will give and bequeath unto the said Dame Dorothy my wife, in full recompence of all claims challenges and demands, which she may make unto my goods, chattels or moveables whatsoever, either by common law, custom or otherwise after my decease, (and in consideration she shall refuse to take, nor shall take any other benefit or profit use or commodity of my said goods or chattels, other than I shall give limit and appoint by this my last will and testament) all her Jewells Chains Bracelets, pearls, buttons of gold and pearl, aglets and rings which she has now in her possession. And I give her all her wearing apparel whatsoever. And as much of my plate which I now have at my house called Frobisher hall in Altofts in the county of York, as shall amount to the value of two hundred pounds, the one half thereof in silver plate valued at five shillings the ounce and the other half to be parcel gilt, at six shillings the ounce in value.........".

This extract shows that a Will is a very valuable document in understanding the way of life of people in the past. The Will goes on to leave Dorothy the beds, linen, furniture etc in Frobisher Hall and all the household items at his house at Walthamstowe in Essex, also his two coaches with their furniture and his two white horses and the choice of all his other horses, mares, geldings and colts. He left her ten milk cows, half his flock of sheep and the residue of all his other moveables, chattels and implements that he had not identified for others. He made Peter Frobisher the son of his deceased elder brother John Frobisher his sole executor and, after bequests to various relatives and friends, including £576 in monetary gifts, he made Peter Frobisher the main beneficiary of the rest of his estate.

Early in the Second World War one of Hitler's bombs landed directly outside the north door of St Giles' Church, Cripplegate, London (the first bomb to fall on London landed very close to St Giles). The blast devastated the fabric of the building and with it the original memorial to Sir Martin. A shower of incendiary bombs followed later and the resulting firestorm was so fierce, and the temperature so intense, that even the cement in the building caught fire and the church was reduced to a skeletal wreck. George Frobisher remembered visiting the church before the war in 1922 and saw the original monument to Martin. When he visited the restored church in the nineteen seventies he was surprised to find that nothing had been done to replace the destroyed monument. In the restoration of the building a new arch had been built over the chancel and two heads were incorporated at its lower ends, one of which represents Sir Martin. It was felt that the original memorial ought to be replaced and, along with his family, his Trust and "The Friends of St Giles", he set about providing a replacement. It was installed on the wall of the south aisle, near to where Sir Martin is buried, and close to John Milton's memorial. It was dedicated on 11th May 1980 and the inscription reads:

> "SIR MARTIN FROBISHER Kt
> OF
> NORMANTON, YORKSHIRE 1535—1594
> INTERRED IN THIS CHURCH
> SEEKER OF THE NORTH-WEST PASSAGE
> 1576-7-8
> FAMED FOR HIS DECISIVE ACTION
> AGAINST
> THE SPANISH ARMADA"

SIR MARTIN FROBISHER.

The present year being the Tercentenary of the Defeat of the Great Spanish Armada, the Vestry of St. Giles, Cripplegate, thought that it would be an opportune time to place a memorial in the Church to one who played such a gallant part in that momentous struggle. The design as shown above has been approved, and the monument is in course of execution. When finished it will be placed on the wall in the south aisle.

Design of the original Frobisher memorial in St Giles' Church, London.

The replacement memorial tablet in St Giles' Church.

In 1988 Plymouth celebrated the 400th anniversary of the defeat of the Armada. The City is rightly proud of its nautical history and the men who have contributed to it. The national memorial monument erected in 1888 celebrating the victory stands proudly on the Hoe. Unfortunately Martin does not enjoy a prominent place on the memorial and his coat of arms is on the base. Records show that in the original design he was to be on the main shaft along with Howard, Raleigh and Drake who along with Martin were the chief commanders but he was displaced in favour of Lord Henry Seymour, who played a minor role in comparison. However he does have a room named after him in the Council offices and a residential block at HMS Drake at Devonport. He is also included in the excellent Dome exhibition on the Hoe. There are also numerous roads and streets named after him, especially at seaside towns. The primary school at Altofts and one of the houses at Normanton Grammar School are named after him.

The National Armada Memorial on Plymouth Hoe.

The frontal of the National Armada Memorial.

The Frobisher accommodation block at HMS Drake,
Devonport, Plymouth.

Martin is also remembered in Canada because of his three
voyages. A town at the head of Frobisher Straits, Baffin Island

was named Frobisher Bay for many years but it has been rightly renamed with an Inuit name, Iqualit. The bay is still called Frobisher Bay. To celebrate the 400th anniversary of the occasion when the Anglican Communion Service was first held in North America a special service was held at St Jude's Cathedral at Iqualit and one can still stay at the Frobisher Inn which overlooks the town. A Canada coin was also minted to mark the anniversary of Martin's voyages of discovery in search of the Northwest Passage. It could be that with global warming and the resulting melting of the ice caps that there will be renewed interest in finding and using this route to China and the East.

St Jude's Cathedral, Iqualit with the Frobisher Inn in the background

400th Anniversary Celebration
of
THE HOLY COMMUNION
According to the Anglican Rite

St. Jude's Cathedral
Frobisher Bay, N.W.T.

Diocese of The Arctic
Anglican Church of Canada

AUGUST 30th

 1578 ◁ᐅᒍᓐ **30** Γ 1978

ᐊᑦᒑᒡ ᓯᕐᐅᖰᐊᐅᓐᐤᒎ ᐅᕐᐅᖰᑯᐤ 400ᑯᐤ
ᒃ ᒍᓇᐅᑯᖅ ᐊᖅᕐᖠᖤᔍᐤ ᐊᒍᖛᑯᑭᖅᖅ
ᐊᖤᒐᑲΓᐅᑦ ᐱᐅᒐᖤᒥᑦ Lᒐᖠᒐᑦ

ᐊᑎᐤ ᐊᖅᖠᖤᖮᑯᒐᖅ ᒍᑲᒐᐤᐳᑐᐸᐊᑎᓐᖴᒐ
ᐊᑲᖒᖟᒐ ᒐᑲᑦᒐᐊΓ

ᐊᖤᑢᖟᒍᐊᐳᖤᖤᖤᐊᑦ ᑲᒥᖝᖟᖴᒐ ᐊᒐᐊᑦ ᒐᑲᖟᒐ
ᐊᖤᒐᑲΓᐅᑦ ᐊᒐΓᖟᒍᖤᑲᒃᒐᑦ ᑲᐊᑦΓ

The 400th Anniversary Service Sheet, St Jude's Cathedral,
Iqaulit

Side 1 of a coin minted in Canada to celebrate Martin Frobisher's voyages in search of the Northwest Passage.

Side 2 of the commemorative coin.

Perhaps the reputation, fame and memory of this "Elizabethan Hero" are best transmitted to and carried forward in the hearts and minds of successive generations of schoolchildren. May their hearts be stirred as they read about his amazing adventures in search of the Northwest Passage and the vital part he played in England's maritime history. Like all human beings Martin Frobisher had many weaknesses and they are evident to us today as well as to his contemporaries. However his undoubted qualities of leadership, courage, and skill, which were so decisive in helping to defeat the Spanish Armada and in building up the influence of England, epitomised his family motto "God himself helps the brave" and are an example to all.

BIBLIOGRAPHY

Peter Padfield, *Armada,* Victor Gollancz, 1988

George Frobisher, *The Frobisher Story,* 1979

Vilhjalmur Stefansson, *The Three Voyages of Martin Frobisher,* The Argonaut Press
Vols 1&2, 1938

Garrett Mattingly, *The Defeat of The Spanish Armada,* The Reprint Society, London, 1961

James McDermott, *Martin Frobisher, Elizabethan Privateer,* Yale University Press, 2001

National Maritime Museum, *ARMADA 1588-1988. The Official Catalogue,* Penguin Books Ltd., 1988

Armada 400, Souvenir Programme, Plymouth, The Evening Herald and Plymouth City Council, 1988

Michael Lewis, *The Spanish Armada,* Pan Books Ltd., 1966

Neville Williams, *The Sea Dogs,* Macmillan Publishing, New York, 1975

Edward Payne, *Voyages of Drake and Gilbert,* Oxford University Press, 1922

W A Kenyon, *Tokens of Possession,* Royal Ontario Museum 1975, University Of Toronto Press.

D D Hogarth, *Mines, Minerals Metallurgy,* Canadian Museum of Civilization, 1994

James Mildren, *The Incredible Armada,* Devon Books, 1988

A L Rowse, *The Expansion of Elizabethan England,* The Reprint Society London, 1957

Royal Armada, 400 Years, Manorial Research (Armada) Ltd., Yale and Valor plc and the National Maritime Museum, Greenwich, 1988

ENDNOTES

1   Vilhmjalmur Stefansson, *The Three Voyages of Martin Frobisher,* Argonaut Press 1938, p.Ixxvi.
2   Stefansson, *op.cit.* p.xcvi.
3   Stefansson, *op.cit.* p.xcvii.
4   Stephanson, *op.cit.* vol I, p.165.
5   Stephenson, *op.cit.* vol.I, p.57.
6   Stefanson, *op.cit.* vol I, p.60.
7   W A Kenyon, *Tokens Of Possession,* Royal Ontario Museum 1975, p. 64.
8   W A Kenyon, *op.cit.* p. 77.
9   Stefansson, *op.cit* vol I, p. 91.
10 Stefansson, *op.cit.* vol I, p. 96.
11 W A Kenyon, *op.cit.* p. 96.
12 Stefansson, *op.cit.* vol I, p. 122.
13 George Frobisher, *The Frobisher Story,* p. 46.
14 Stefansson, *op.cit.* vol 2, p. 48.
15 Stefansson, *op.cit.* vol 2, p. 123.
16 Stefansson, *op.cit.* vol 2, p. 124.
17 James McDermott, *op.cit.* vol 2, p. 265.
18 Edward Payne & C R Beazley, *Voyages of Drake & Gilbert,* Oxford—Clarenden Press 1922, p.255.
19 Peter Padfield, *Armada,* Victor Gollancz 1988, p. 44.
20 Peter Padfield, *op.cit.* p. 58.
21 J K Laughton Ed., *State Papers Relating to the Defeat of the Spanish Armada 1,* Naval Records 1894, pp. 148-49.
22 George Frobisher, *op.cit.* 1979, p. 20.

23   James McDermott, *op.cit*, p. 364

24   Peter Padfield, *op.cit.* p. 128.

25   Peter Padfield, *op.cit.* p. 128.

26   James McDermott, *op.cit.* p365

27   Michael Lewis, *The Spanish Armada*, Pan Books Ltd. 1960, p. 188.

28   Garrett Mattingly, *The Defeat Of The Spanish Armada*, The Reprint Society, London, 1959, p. 328.

29   George Frobisher, *op.cit.* p. 47.

30   James McDermott, *op.cit.* p. 417.

31   James McDermott, *op.cit.* p. 418.

32   George Frobisher, *op.cit.* p. 21.

33   George Frobisher, *op.cit.* p. 21